Jacob Lawrence

THE MIGRATION SERIES

Jacob Lawrence
THE MIGRATION SERIES

Edited by Elizabeth Hutton Turner

Introductory essay by Henry Louis Gates, Jr.

Essays by Lonnie G. Bunch III and Spencer R. Crew, Patricia Hills, Elizabeth Steele and Susana M. Halpine, Jeffrey C. Stewart, Diane Tepfer, and Deborah Willis
Chronology by Stephen Bennett Phillips

THE RAPPAHANNOCK PRESS
in association with The Phillips Collection, Washington, D.C. 1993

Published on the occasion of the exhibition "Jacob Lawrence: The *Migration* Series," organized by The Phillips Collection, Washington, D.C.

The exhibition and its national tour are sponsored by Philip Morris Companies Inc.

Additional support has been provided by the National Endowment for the Humanities, the Henry Luce Foundation, Inc., and the National Endowment for the Arts.

EXHIBITION ITINERARY

The Phillips Collection, Washington, D.C.
September 23, 1993–January 9, 1994

Milwaukee Art Museum, Milwaukee, Wisconsin
January 28–March 20, 1994

Portland Art Museum, Portland, Oregon
April 19–June 12, 1994

Birmingham Museum of Art, Birmingham, Alabama
July 10–September 4, 1994

Saint Louis Art Museum, St. Louis, Missouri
September 30–November 27, 1994

The Museum of Modern Art, New York
January 11, 1994–April 11, 1995

LIBRARY OF CONGRESS CATALOGING-IN-PUBLICATION DATA
Jacob Lawrence : the migration series / edited by Elizabeth Hutton
  Turner ; introduction by Henry Louis Gates, Jr. ; essays by Lonnie
  G. Bunch ... [et al.].
    p. cm.
  Includes bibliographical references and index.
  ISBN 0–9636129–0–5 (hc) ISBN 0–9636129–1–3 (pb)
  1. Lawrence, Jacob, 1917–   —Criticism and interpretation.
2. Afro-Americans in art. I. Turner, Elizabeth Hutton, 1952–
II. Bunch, Lonnie G.
  ND237.L29J23   1993
  759.13—dc20   93-1402
                                                        CIP

Edited by Ellen Cochran Hirzy
Designed by Bruce Campbell
Typeset by The Sarabande Press
Manufactured in Italy by Sfera, Milan

Cover: Jacob Lawrence, "During the World War there was a great migration North by southern Negroes," panel 1, *The Migration of the Negro*, 1940–41 (The Phillips Collection)

Frontispiece: "The migration gained momentum," detail of panel 18, *The Migration of the Negro*, 1940–41 (The Museum of Modern Art)

Contents

The Henry Luce Foundation is pleased to support this landmark exhibition at The Phillips Collection. "Jacob Lawrence: The *Migration* Series" reunites, for the first time in twenty years, one of Lawrence's most significant and powerful accomplishments.

This monumental sixty-panel work chronicles a milestone in American social history—the African American population shift from the rural South to the industrial North. In exploring its causes and effects, Lawrence captured a broad and challenging range of subjects in his uniquely evocative style.

The catalogue illustrates this series in its entirety for the first time since its creation in 1940–41. It is a fitting coincidence that it was in *Fortune* magazine that these works made their printed debut in 1941.

I am pleased to count this exhibition as the latest project of the Luce Foundation's Program in American Art, which has supported, since 1982, over one hundred exhibitions and catalogues in some sixty-five museums. And I am delighted to join The Phillips Collection for a second time in this way.

Henry Luce III
Chairman and CEO
The Henry Luce Foundation, Inc.

"I don't think about this series in terms of history. I think in terms of contemporary life. It was such a part of me I didn't think of something outside. . . . It was a portrait of myself, a portrait of my family, a portrait of my peers. . . . It was like a still life with bread, a still life with flowers. It was like a landscape you see."

—Jacob Lawrence

Foreword

This exhibition commemorates an important moment in the history of American painting, in the history of The Phillips Collection and The Museum of Modern Art, and in the history of this country.

In December 1941 the art dealer Edith Halpert exhibited a group of sixty paintings by Jacob Lawrence in her Downtown Gallery in New York. The series, which Lawrence titled *The Migration of the Negro*, illustrates the movement of African Americans from the farms and rural communities of the South to the industrialized cities of the North and the Midwest where they hoped to find better work and a better life. Halpert planned the exhibition as part of a much larger project to focus the attention of the segregated New York art world upon contemporary African American artists. She had arranged for a consortium of dealers to simultaneously exhibit the work of a number of artists included in Alain Locke's recently published book, *The Negro in Art*. Unfortunately, Pearl Harbor was attacked the day before the scheduled gala opening, and Halpert's grand plan collapsed. Nevertheless, the Downtown Gallery proceeded to show the *Migration* series.

The exhibition gave Halpert an opportunity to bring the series to the attention of both Duncan Phillips and Alfred Barr, the director of The Museum of Modern Art. As a result, *The Migration of the Negro* was exhibited at The Phillips Collection in February 1942. Both museums had expressed an interest in purchasing the series, and in March Halpert arranged for them to divide the acquisition of the sixty panels. Apparently, Adele Rosenwald Levy, a trustee and benefactor of The Museum of Modern Art, so admired the stairway depicted in panel no. 46 that Barr requested all of the even-numbered paintings. Duncan Phillips happily agreed to acquire the odd-numbered works.

Phillips, like most critics of the time, was impressed by Lawrence's distinctive combination of abstraction with socially relevant subject matter. He was no doubt aware of the significance of incorporating Lawrence's unique palette and patterns into his ever-expanding definition of American modernism. In Phillips's correspondence there are no references to matters of race, although Lawrence's works were among the first by African American artists to enter the collection. Barr, on the other hand, acknowledged to Halpert that Lawrence's panels were the first works by an artist of African American descent to enter the collection of The Museum of Modern Art. No doubt Phillips and Barr both recognized that while the series focused on the recent migration of African Americans from South to North, it also addressed matters of migration and immigration that are part of the experience of the nation as a whole.

Even with the benefit of more than fifty years of hindsight, many people continue to be astonished that the "migration" of the work of African American artists into our nation's important collections of modern and contemporary art reflects the greater issues of segregation and racism that have plagued this country throughout the twentieth century. In this connection it is interesting that in 1942, with the fight for civil rights hailed as the second front in World War II, The Museum of Modern Art organized a national tour of *The Migration of the Negro* and presented the series as an anti-fascist statement. The show remained on the road for two years and returned to New York in 1944 for a final engagement at the Museum of Modern Art.

The Migration of the Negro was not reunited again until 1971, in the aftermath of the unprecedented activity of the civil rights movement, when it was brought together again at The Museum of Modern Art in an exhibition titled "The Artist as Adversary." The show was also held at The Phillips Collection in 1972, but otherwise it did not travel. Apparently because of a lack of funding, the exhibition was not accompanied by a catalogue at either venue.

The current exhibition of *The Migration of the Negro* has been organized by The Phillips Collection in conjunction with an interdisciplinary team of scholars who have studied Lawrence's narrative from the vantage points of art, history, criticism, and literature. More than fifty years after the creation of the series, a new generation of scholars has gathered the necessary texts and sources to retrieve, revitalize, and re-create Lawrence's original vision. This catalogue offers both a compendium of scholarly analysis and, many will be surprised to learn, the first complete visual record of the series.

The exhibition is the result of a two-year planning process that benefited from the work of many, especially the members of the principal team who were brought together and led by associate curator Elizabeth Hutton Turner: Lonnie G. Bunch III, Spencer R. Crew, Henry Louis Gates, Jr., Patricia Hills, Richard J. Powell, James E. Sims, Connie Spinner, Jeffrey C. Stewart, Diane Tepfer, and Deborah Willis. In addition, Jacob Lawrence himself participated in much of the planning. With his characteristic selflessness and generosity, he imparted a wealth of information and made himself available throughout the process. We are enormously grateful to all for their kindness, cooperation, and commitment to the project.

We are deeply indebted to the Henry Luce Foundation for its generous funding of many of the educational and outreach programs for the exhibition as well as the didactic and documentary aspects of the installation. The Luce Foundation's outstanding record of assistance for publications, exhibitions, and projects devoted to American art is widely recognized, and The Phillips Collection is once again honored by the foundation's support. Without it, we could not have presented much of the contextual and historical material that so significantly augments and enriches our experience of the *Migration* series.

In addition, I would like to express the profound gratitude of The Phillips Collection for the exceedingly generous support of the Philip Morris Companies Inc., the sponsor of the exhibition. Philip Morris's long and distinguished record of support for exhibitions is well known to museum visitors. Over the years the company has sponsored many of the greatest exhibitions we have seen in this country. Once again, we are deeply indebted to Philip Morris for their outstanding patronage and exceptional record of commitment to the arts.

Charles S. Moffett
Director
The Phillips Collection

Acknowledgments

This catalogue and exhibition would not be possible without the help and cooperation of many people and institutions. I am extremely grateful for their good will and their generous contributions to the successful completion of this project.

First and foremost, I want to thank Jacob and Gwen Lawrence for their guidance and support in making this exhibition a reality.

The early commitment of the National Endowment for the Humanities in the form of a planning grant enabled us to assemble an impressive panel of consultants to address the many issues this exhibition would raise. We are very grateful to the Philip Morris Companies Inc. for their strong financial support, which made the realization of our planning and the national tour possible. Important additional support has been provided by the Henry Luce Foundation, Inc., and the National Endowment for the Arts, to which we are also grateful.

I also want to acknowledge the extraordinary generosity and cooperation of The Museum of Modern Art, particularly Kirk Varnedoe, director, and Cora Rosevear, associate curator, Department of Painting and Sculpture, in agreeing to lend the museum's thirty panels and to host the reunion of the series in New York. Osa Brown, director of publications, and her assistant Darla Decker helped in many ways; Kate Keller, photographer, supplied the transparencies of the works; and Victoria Garvin provided research assistance. Susan Bates, loan assistant, and Anna Hillen, senior registrar assistant, also facilitated the museum's loan.

Our planning team helped us turn the story of the *Migration* series into an exhibition. They all deserve warm thanks: Jacob and Gwen Lawrence; Lonnie G. Bunch III, chair, Department of Social and Cultural History, National Museum of American History, Smithsonian Institution; Spencer R. Crew, acting director, National Museum of American History; Henry Louis Gates, Jr., W.E.B. Du Bois Professor of the Humanities and chair of the Afro-American Studies Department, Harvard University; Patricia Hills, professor of art history, Boston University; Richard J. Powell, assistant professor, Department of Art and Art History, Duke University; James E. Sims, director, Museum Services Project, Office of International Relations, Smithsonian Institution; Connie Spinner, Center for Educational Change; Jeffrey C. Stewart, assistant professor of history, George Mason University; Diane Tepfer, assistant curator, Prints and Photographs Division, Library of Congress; and Deborah Willis, museum specialist, African American Museum Project, Smithsonian Institution.

I also would like to thank the many kind and dedicated individuals who facilitated our efforts to secure photographs, documentation, and references: Mary Ison, head of reference section, Prints and Photographs Division, and Dennis McNew, head of public services, Photoduplication Division, Library of Congress; Kimberly Cody and Maricia Battle, National Museum of American Art, Smithsonian Institution; Ann Potter, Archives of American Art, Smithsonian Institution; Nicholas Natanson, National Archives; Mikki Carpenter and Rona Roob, Museum of Modern Art; Frederick Stielow, executive director, and Andrew Simons, reference archivist, Amistad Research Center; National Portrait Gallery, Smithsonian Institution; Barbara Hillman, New York Public Library; Tammi Lawson, Schomburg Center for Research in Black Culture; Philippe Alexandre, Terry Dintenfass Gallery; Donna Mussenden Van Der Zee; Joseph Solomon, executor, Estate of Carl Van Vechten; Georgette Seabrook Powell; Louis Faurer; Philip J. and Suzanne Schiller; and Stone Wiske, Maryemma Graham, and Katherine A. Viator, Educational Technology Center, Harvard Graduate School of Education. Thanks also go to Edward Owen for his color transparencies for the Migration panels in The Phillips Collection and for his copy prints.

I have benefited enormously from the advice, assistance, cooperation, and support of the team of scholars whose collaborative effort has resulted in this book: Lonnie G. Bunch III, Spencer Crew, Henry Louis Gates, Jr., Susana Halpine, Patricia Hills, Elizabeth Steele, Jeffrey Stewart, Diane Tepfer, and Deborah Willis. I also want to thank Richard Powell for his careful reading of the manuscript and Karen Schneider for her meticulous proofreading. Ellen Cochran Hirzy is to be commended for her thoughtful editing. I am also grateful to Susan Ralston, consulting editor, and to Rappahannock Press.

I extend my warmest appreciation to Stanley Staniski, who translated this story into a powerful video.

Last but not least, I offer my heartfelt thanks to all the staff at The Phillips Collection who have adopted this project with insight, enthusiasm, and hard work. Above all, I am immensely grateful to: Elisabeth Foxley Leach, researcher; Stephen B. Phillips, assistant curator for administrative affairs; Elizabeth Chew, assistant curator; and Sarah Anne Morgan and Patricia Richmond, interns, Curatorial Department. I am also grateful to: Donna McKee, education director; Helen Santini, assistant education director; William Koberg, installations manager; Joseph Holbach, registrar; Beverly Balger and Rebecca Dodson, assistant registrars; Shelley Wischhusen-Treece, chief preparator; Jim Whitelaw, preparator; Karen Schneider, librarian; Laura Lester, director of public affairs; Kristin Krathwohl, public information officer; Joyce Dull, public affairs assistant; Andrea Barnes, membership/special events coordinator; Ignacio Moreno, visual resources director; Penny Saffer, director of development; Cathy Card Sterling, director of corporate and foundation relations; Catherine Augenstein, grants coordinator; Tom Gilleylen, building services manager; Frank Hartman, assistant manager for facilities; Elizabeth Redisch, museum shop manager; Jose Tain-Alfonso, administrator; Norman Gugliotta, accountant; and Brion Elliot, assistant to the controller. Finally, I would like to thank Charles Moffett, director, Eliza Rathbone, chief curator, and Laughlin Phillips, chairman of the board of trustees, for their unfailing support throughout the preparation of this exhibition.

Elizabeth Hutton Turner
Curator of the Exhibition

Jacob Lawrence. *One-Way Ticket*, 1948, ink on paper (collection of Jacob Lawrence and Gwendolyn Knight Lawrence). Illustration for Langston Hughes's *One-Way Ticket*, 1948

Introduction

ELIZABETH HUTTON TURNER

I pick up my life
And take it with me
And I put it down in
Chicago, Detroit, Buffalo, Scranton,
Any place that is North and East
And not Dixie.

—Langston Hughes, "One-Way Ticket" (1948)

When Jacob Lawrence read Langston Hughes's 1948 ode to the African American migration, he made a drawing. He sketched a waiting room filled with travelers, trunks, and suitcases. Along its perimeter was a line of seated figures whose immense bodies cradled squirming toddlers and babies. This row seemed to go on and on, figure upon figure, profile upon profile, until from above and behind still more milling travelers setting up camps of makeshift seats moved down and closed off the view. Gazing out expectantly from this starkly contrasting sea of anonymous black figures clothed in white, a young boy sat front and center on his suitcase. He witnessed the scene, the significance of which may or may not be explained, perhaps only in retrospect. Why such prominence for a child? Who was this boy who watched and waited?

Jacob Lawrence knew about moving. Born in 1917, he had moved from Atlantic City to Easton, Pennsylvania, to Philadelphia, living in and out of foster homes before settling in Harlem with his mother when he was thirteen. There, in the great nexus of twentieth-century African American culture, he began to piece together the fragmented memories of a journey that had taken his family from South to North. He remembered his mother telling him she was born in Fredericksburg, Virginia, and his father in South Carolina. He remembered his foster parents in Philadelphia talking about "another family coming up" and about giving clothing and coal to the new arrivals. His teachers in Harlem explained what caused these people to leave the land, leave the planters, leave the tenant farms, and come to live in city tenements and work in factories. He remembered his own

surprise at arriving in Harlem and seeing eight-story buildings with fire escapes like ladders going into the sky.

At first Lawrence had no words, only patterns and colors, to attach to these experiences and memories. Later he began to articulate his own connection with the ongoing struggle of African Americans against injustice and discrimination as he studied under the painter Charles Alston and read accounts of the migration by W.E.B. Du Bois, Carter Woodson, and Emmett J. Scott. Then he could see and describe its effects plainly, even in the portrayals of street-corner orators and vaudeville actors. Such awareness of community empowered Jacob Lawrence to become an artist.

Jacob Lawrence painted *The Migration of the Negro* in 1941. He was twenty-three. His portrayals of Toussaint L'Ouverture, Frederick Douglass, and Harriet Tubman had already earned him a certain reputation as a history painter. The *Migration*, a contemporary narrative, represented a new, far bolder point of departure. Here was the story of an ongoing exodus of black labor, begun at the time of World War I, that was central to the development of African American culture and political freedom. In 1941 the movement was totally invisible to most Americans. Farm Security Administration documentaries of the 1930s, with their fixed focus on conditions in the South and the Midwest, had virtually missed it. The Photo League's Harlem Document had captured only a part—the negative aspect, some would say—of the story.

In Lawrence's hands, the migration became an epic, something comprehensive, timely, and timeless. His words and images conveyed metaphors of injustice, strife, struggle,

Jacob Lawrence, age six, with his mother Rose Lee Armstead Lawrence, his brother William Hale, and his sister Geraldine, 1923

have been monumental, like those by Aaron Douglas, which were placed with honor at the Schomburg Collection during the 1930s. But Lawrence had played only a minor part in the Work Projects Administration. At age twenty-one he was, in his words, "too young for a wall." In any case, by 1941 Lawrence's story had become too big for a wall and his form too radical, too far from traditional constraints to be affixed in one time or space.

Lawrence's vision was completed in multiples of horizontal and vertical panels of the same size, small-scaled and portable, painted with tempera on masonite. There were sixty in all. Lawrence saw no need for frames at the time. Each panel had a painted border ready-made for presentation. Like story boards for a film, they were numbered and sequenced by scene with an accompanying script. Beginning and ending in a train station, the action unfolded in rhythmic progression from painting to painting, with clear stopping points or pauses along the way. Abstracted, expressive figures with exaggerated, masklike features acted out causes and consequences in shallow stagelike spaces. By the time the next train arrived in the sequence, there were still more reasons to get on board. Despite the great range of subjects and settings, a consistent palette of blue-green, orange, yellow, and gray-brown, like clay slip, ensured the visual integrity of the entire assemblage. In fact, unity and consistency were so important to Lawrence that he would not paint the *Migration* series until he had obtained a fellowship from the Rosenwald Fund and used it to secure studio space large enough to lay out all sixty panels and paint them, color by color, all at once.

Lawrence wrote in his Rosenwald application that he hoped to have the *Migration* series completed so that it could be exhibited in the fall of 1941 and later reproduced in a book. He left those arrangements up to others. In a rapid succession of events, Lawrence and the *Migration* series were launched in the New York art world. Critic Alain Locke brought the panels to the Harlem Community Art Center to show dealer Edith Halpert. Halpert, in turn, made them known to the editors of *Fortune* magazine, which published twenty-six of them in November 1941. The next month, Halpert exhibited the series at her Downtown Gallery. Two museums vying for the series—The Museum of Modern Art and The Phillips Memorial Gallery—resolved the issue by each purchasing thirty alternating panels. By the fall

change, hope, ambition, and even beauty. For Lawrence found beauty in struggle. His text, which he carefully researched and wrote before he ever made an image, clearly explained why people needed to leave and were still leaving. It described their hopes for something better, depicted the violence and disease they endured, pointed out their strengths and their potential for political power. Told on the eve of World War II, as American industry once again extended its invitation to black labor, Lawrence's history of the migration was also a cautionary tale, citing disappointments of the recent past and inspiring new hope for the future.

Had Lawrence been born a generation earlier, perhaps he would have become a muralist. Perhaps his images would of 1942, the *Migration* series embarked on a two-year national tour.

Where was Lawrence during this remarkable time? He had gone south for the first time in his life. Hard at work on yet another series, Lawrence was, in his words, "conducting research." In November 1941 he received his copy of *Fortune* on Bienville Avenue in New Orleans. In March 1942 he was in Lenexa, Virginia, visiting his mother's family while final negotiations with Alfred Barr and Duncan Phillips were taking place. Only on his return to New York in June 1942 did he fully realize that he and his message had broken through the color barrier and that two worlds—two very separate, very segregated worlds—had somehow met in agreement about his talent and his vision.

The reunion of Jacob Lawrence's *Migration* series in 1993 provides a great opportunity to revisit the context of its creation. Lawrence himself, for the first time, has dictated the arrangement and installation of the series. He has also revised the text accompanying the images for the purposes of this new exhibition. The scholars contributing to this catalogue explore the multifaceted aspects of the artist and his narrative. We examine how Lawrence—as historian, as researcher, as artist, as *griot*—teaches us to see the migration through painting. The roles of Alain Locke and Edith Halpert are also evaluated. A long-overdue art historical analysis of the series as both image and text is included, and for the first time the series is reproduced in color in its entirety.

Jacob Lawrence is without bitterness but filled and fired with the truth of his story. He, like the boy sitting on the suitcase, holds the legacy of the migration. He discloses it in a vital and vibrant portrait of himself and his experience. Above all, his highly original words, forms, and colors show him unafraid to "sing a new song."

Jacob Lawrence, ca. 1941 (National Archives, Harmon Foundation Collection)

New Negroes, Migration, and Cultural Exchange

HENRY LOUIS GATES, JR.

World-wide dusk
Of dear dark faces
Driven before an alien wind,
Scattered like seed
From far-off places
Growing in soil
That's strange and thin,
Hybrid plants
In another's garden.

— Langston Hughes, "Black Seed," 1930

A new type of Negro is evolving—a city Negro.
He is being evolved out of those strangely
divergent elements of the general background.
And this is a fact overlooked by those students
of human behavior. . . .
In ten years, Negroes have been actually
transported from one culture to another.

— Charles S. Johnson, 1925

The great movement of people of African descent from the rural South to the urban North between 1900 and 1930 was the largest movement of black bodies since slavery radically abstracted black Africans from Senegambia and Ghana to Angola, from River Nigeria to the Congo, and then removed them to South America, the West Indies, and the agriculture-dominated southern United States. Just as slavery inadvertently created a new "African" culture—a New World Western, Pan-African culture and ethnicity—so, too, did the Great Migration create a new culture—a cross-pollinated black culture, one northern and urban yet thoroughly southern in its roots. As much as anything else, the Great Migration was a site of cultural contestation, a new exchange and synthesis of black cultures once separate and isolated. The sheer energy of this dynamic process of acculturation— the exchange and grafting of southern and northern, urban and rural—resulted in two of the most important cultural movements of the twentieth century—the Jazz Age and the Harlem, or New Negro, Renaissance. While musicians and writers, from Langston Hughes to Duke Ellington, from Jean Toomer to Don Redman, documented the synthesis, it would be Jacob Lawrence's great achievement to register this monumental movement of economics and aesthetics in the visual realm.

Lawrence's *Migration* series is an attempt to resolve the two central competing modes of representation in the African American tradition that clashed and struggled for dominance in the 1920s and 1930s: a naturalism that sought to reveal how individual "choice" was always shaped and curtailed by environmental forces and a modernism that sought to chart the relation of the individual will to the chaotic environment. He turned to an "expressive cubism," as Patricia Hills has called it, a figural modernism that employed an extended narrative technique to settle the inherent tension between these two poles. The result is a new, mediating form of representation, an extended artwork of epic proportions. Its sole counterpart in the black literary tradition is Richard Wright's *Native Son*, a deeply naturalistic work, dense in its determinism, concerned with the aftermath of the migration. As for representing the *process* of migration, there is no literary equivalent to Lawrence's visual narrative.

"To migrate" means to extend a "habitat gradually from an old into a new region" and "to move from one site to another in a host organism, especially as part of a life cycle." The word stems from the Latin *migratus*, "to change," and peripherally from the Sanskrit word *mayate*, "he exchanges." Lawrence brilliantly evokes this sense of exchange through the use of ladders, stairs, or railroad tracks as a leitmotif (panels 36, 38, 39, 46). Although there had been other migrations—the "Exodusters" to Kansas after the collapse of Reconstruction in 1876 and black southerners to the North beginning at the turn of the century—in 1910 no less than 75 percent of all African Americans lived in rural areas, and 90 percent lived in the South. But by 1920 almost 40 percent of the northern black population lived in eight cities: Chicago, Detroit, New York, Cleveland, Cincinnati, Columbus, Philadelphia, and Pittsburgh.

There were as many reasons for migration as there were people who migrated. Most obvious, of course, was that since slavery the North had been a literal haven of freedom to which the slave could escape, giving it mythic proportions. "Down South," on the other hand, a thermidorian reaction followed the short-lived Reconstruction period. A Sisyphean sharecropper system quickly emerged as a substitute form of economic slavery. White supremacy was codified into a cruel legal system, and systematically untrammeled mass aggression was visited upon the black. During this period, America's own Dark Ages, more black people were lynched, burned, and tortured than at any other time in the nation's history. Blacks fled.

The statistics are revealing: Between 1870 and 1890, an average of 41,378 people migrated each decade from the South. Between 1890 and 1900, however, more than twice that number migrated—107,796 people. Between 1890 and 1910, the black populations of New Jersey, Pennsylvania, and Illinois more than doubled; that of New York nearly tripled.

A veil of blackness covered the North, especially Harlem. As Gilbert Osofsky shows in his important study, *Harlem: The Making of A Ghetto*, between 1910 and 1920 the black population of New York increased sixty-six percent, and between 1920 and 1930 it expanded 115 percent. Another type of migration occurred at the same time: between 1920 and 1930, 118,792 white people left Harlem, while 87,417 black people arrived. (Still, by 1930 no less than 80 percent of Harlem businesses were white owned.)

While works such as Wright's *Native Son* and Ralph Ellison's *Invisible Man* draw on the post-migration period for their settings, migration as a theme in black literature is fairly rare. But the drama of migration captured the imagination of an entire people for more than half a century. Whole families just picked up what they could carry—and often what they couldn't—and left their homes and friends, many times in the middle of the night, for the hope of the unfamiliar. For the migrant, the move often meant the difference between life and death in one form or another. For all, however,

migration initiated them into the technological America of the twentieth century as if they had been transported in a time machine. And this movement through time and space often had tragic consequences. As Langston Hughes wrote in "Po' Boy Blues" (1932):

> When I was home de
>   Sunshine seemed like gold.
> When I was home de
>   Sunshine seemed like gold.
> Since I cam North de
>   Whole damn world's turned cold.

As the urban black population swelled, it was imperative to the political goals of socioeconomic integration and cultural assimilation (embraced by such organizations as the NAACP and the Urban League) that separate communities of black people, and especially Harlem, be perceived as "normal" communities, not tainted in any way by such a massive gathering of black folk. James Weldon Johnson in 1930 was careful to explain that, quite unlike ordinary concentrations of blacks, "Negro Harlem is situated in the heart of Manhattan and covers one of the most beautiful and healthful sites in the whole city. It is not a fringe, it is not a slum, nor is it a 'quarter' consisting of dilapidated tenements." And Johnson's testament was only one in a chorus.

But in the midst of the New Negro spiritual awakening led by the talented tenth or the "cultured few" were human beings living in Harlem, which was rapidly becoming a rotting slum. The chairman of a New York City housing committee remarked in 1927 that the socioeconomic conditions in Harlem were "deplorable," "unspeakable," "incredible." "The State," he said, "would not allow cows to live in some of these apartments used by colored people." The Harlem death rate was 42 percent higher than that of the entire city. Twice as many black mothers died in childbirth as did mothers in other districts. The infant mortality rate in Harlem was twice that of the rest of New York. Undertaking was the most profitable business.

As early as 1913, George Edmund Haynes wrote that "there is growing up in the cities of America a distinct Negro world," one "isolated from many of the impulses of the common life and little understood by the white world." This world grew even more distinct as blacks from the rural South migrated in greater numbers to the urban North. This was the

Harlem of which James Weldon Johnson could say, "It is the Mecca for . . . the talented of the entire Negro world." This was the Harlem, Langston Hughes wrote,

> where from bar to bar
> where from glass to glass
> I drowned my paid
> right to the dance-floor
> trodden and worn with steps
> with stomps
> with slows
> with songs
> with sons
> with blues.

The juxtaposition of glamorous image and stark reality is basic to an understanding of exactly why the Harlem Renaissance could not sustain itself as a cultural movement. While "slumming parties" frequented Harlem cabarets to soak up some "African" rhythm, while white intellectuals waxed eloquent over Harlem's exoticism and eroticism, while propagandists black and white pictured the ghetto as a mythical dreamland north of Central Park, Harlem became one of the most appalling slums in the country. "Had these people [from downtown] arrived at noon and inspected a rat-infested tenement," Osofsky writes, "their image of the gay Negro might have been changed; yet American racial consciousness refused to recognize any but the supposedly joyous side of Negro culture. It was impossible to mobilize any massive support for racial reform in the 1920s because American society voluntarily blinded itself to the harsh realities of Negro existence."

What caused the ghettoes? How could an entire neighborhood deteriorate into a slum? Osofsky argues that the primary economic factor was the astronomical increase in rent brought about by increased settlement in a restricted residential area. Because he could not escape to another, integrated neighborhood, the black tenant had to pay these exorbitant rents—by 1927, nearly double the 1919 figure.

Black people invaded the North, full of hope and energy, only to encounter the Great Depression in 1929. The depression, which was to destroy and create so many American institutions with its sorrow and deprivation, had attacked Harlem early in the 1920s. "The reason why the Depression didn't have the impact on the Negroes that it had

on the whites," George Schuyler wrote, "was that Negroes had been in the Depression all the time." The thin veneer of the Black Mecca, the glamour of Black Paris, when scraped away by the depression revealed a deep structure of rot. Very few writers and artists addressed themselves to the socioeconomic conditions until the depression, preferring instead to focus on the sense of possibility that migration promised. In their works of art, they were almost as separated from the reality of black America's daily existence as were the whites who emigrated each night from downtown; the latter had an excuse, perhaps, but the former did not. But Jacob Lawrence succeeded marvelously in the realm of the visual precisely where the New Negro writers faulted.

What the Great Migration meant for African American culture specifically and American culture generally can scarcely be described. A regional, parochial black culture became cosmopolitan and universal, especially in its musical forms. The blues split into two distinct but related forms, the classic blues and "country" blues. Ragtime, in the rich cauldron of the migrating 1920s, metamorphosed itself into something called "jazz." The Negro people suddenly were of two sorts, "old" and "new." African Americans *reinvented* themselves, as more than a million souls removed themselves from the provinces to the metropole, from the periphery to the center, from South to North, from agriculture to industrial, from rural to urban, from the nineteenth century to the twentieth. The greatest transformation of all, of course, was a "new" Negro culture, the outcome of the exchange of traditional southern and northern black cultures and the resulting synthesis of the two. Jacob Lawrence's masterful visual narration of the most significant development in African American history since the Civil War is both product and record of this transformation. While the black visual tradition was exceptionally rich and varied by the 1930s, no artist before Lawrence had undertaken a *narrative* series of a historical event from the black past.

In fact, the false optimism of the New Negro writers found its counterpart in the idealized black images and the neoprimitivism (with its faux-African motifs) that permeate so much of black art in the 1920s. Artists and writers alike were reacting to a long history of racist stereotyping of the black figure—especially between 1890 and 1920—by creating ideal images of a transcendent African and neo-African nobility. To call the Harlem Renaissance a "New Negro" movement is to describe exactly what its visual and verbal artists sought to create: a largely unregistered, unimagined image of the Noble Negro that would destroy forever the confusing, limited range of black stereotypes that every artist had to confront. Lawrence's figural modernism, his "expressive cubism," allowed him to capture the tension between the energy and potential of migration as well as its often tragic consequences.

Migration for Lawrence was most aptly symbolized in the recurring figure of the ladder, which signifies a bridge or a conduit, a connection between the past and the future as well as between the South and the North. Whereas the visual meaning associated with ladders in the black tradition suggests vertical or hierarchical patterns of progressive movement—"lifting as we climb," as the motto of a prominent black women's organization had it—Lawrence's use of the image is much more subtle. His ladder is a span, a connecting mechanism, the very linkage of the chain of tradition, of the old with the new.

Lawrence is quite eloquent about the levels of signification in the series and about his motivation and inspiration to paint it: "I was part of the migration, as was my family: my mother, my sister, and my brother. . . . I grew up hearing tales about people 'coming up,' another family arriving. People who'd been . . . in the North for a few years, they would say another family 'came up' and they would help them to get established . . . by giving them clothes and fuel and things of that sort . . . . I was only about 10, 11, or 12. It was the '20s. . . . And of course there was a great deal of tension throughout the country—the ethnic tension and so on—I guess you have a similar situation today. But this was all new to me. I was a youngster and I heard these stories over and over again. . . . I didn't realize that we were even a part of that. . . . I didn't realize what was happening until about the middle of the 1930s, and that's when the *Migration* series began to take form in my mind."

But what gave rise to Lawrence's extensive use of narrative forms in the series? "By this time I was in Harlem," he says. "I decided to paint this series—I wasn't thinking of sales or of a gallery. I liked storytelling. I went to the Schomburg Library and selected events from South and North. I think that the series alternates from South to North. I just got into it. I didn't separate it—I wasn't looking at it from the inside

out or the outside in. This was such a part of my life. . . . We—my wife Gwen and I—gessoed the panels and got them in order—and I just started doing it. In retrospect now, I think my central concept was, 'people on the move.' I guess that's what migration means. . . . You think of trains and buses and people just on the move. Of course, I was doing research at the time. I guess it was both emotional and intellectual."

One of the most curious aspects of the series to our generation is its open depiction of class tensions within the black community—the clash between the old and the new, the lower migrating classes and the more stable middle classes. Of this, Lawrence responds that "there was a great deal of elitism and snobbery [but] there wasn't one kind of treatment. You'd had blacks living in the North for years since the turn of the century, . . . and many of the blacks coming up from the . . . rural areas of the South were almost illiterate. I imagine—I only can imagine this now—that the treatment was one of compassion at times. So it was a mixture."

Did migration lead to the creation of a self-contained Negro world, since the series seems to be founded primarily upon the lives of black people? "I lived in Harlem. I grew up in Harlem. My life was in the Harlem community. I didn't go outside [it] except to go to an art gallery or a museum. Everything was right there. . . . I remember the *Amsterdam News*—almost every week, there would be a headline: 'Black Accosted,' 57th Street, 42nd Street. [When] you were outside the community, the police could be pretty mean and pretty brutal. You'd be beaten up except if you were a domestic or a janitor. If you went downtown wearing a suit, you could be accosted. We didn't go outside the community, people like myself. Not that we constantly had this fear, but it was there.

"I wouldn't make the qualification that it was better. It was *different*. It was a more cohesive community. You got to know the people on the streets—not by name—but seeing the faces over and over again when you went to church community centers, saw the teachers in the community, interacted with librarians in the community. This is what inspired me. As I talk now, I think that this is a result of that kind of rapport."

How did Lawrence arrive at his particular color scheme to symbolize this transformation of black culture? "We lived in a deep depression. Not only my mother, but the poor people in general. In order to add something to their lives, they decorated their tenements and their homes in all of these colors. I've been asked, Is anybody in my family artistically inclined? I've always felt ashamed of my response and I always said no, not realizing that my artistic sensibility came from this ambiance. I did have this influence, but I didn't realize it was taking place. It's only in retrospect that I realized that I was surrounded by art. You'd walk Seventh Avenue and look in the windows and you'd see all these colors in the depth of the depression. All these colors. You'd walk through Harlem and go to the Apollo Theater, and the jokes that were being told! The pathos! People would laugh, but it was comedy on a very profound, deep, philosophical level. But you can only see this, you can only realize this, in retrospect." In effect, then, Lawrence's sense of color is communal, his way of seeing cultural—"through my mother's way of seeing," he says, "and my mother's friends, her contemporaries, my peers. That's the way it was."

How did Lawrence go about conceiving of ways to represent migration? "I'm seeing the works for the first time in a number of years and I realize now in looking at them that every time I see them, I see them from a different point of view. I notice the symbols. I didn't realize that there were so *many* symbols of railroad stations, bus stations, people traveling! But that's what migration is. You think in terms of people on the move, people moving from one situation to another. . . . Crossroads, bus stations, and train stations— moments of transition—it certainly was a moment of transition in the history of America and for the race. It's one of the big movements in our country. And I want to say this, too: I don't think the blacks in making a movement just contributed to their own development. It contributed to *American* development. Look at your structure of the cities— the passion, the energy, the vitality. Not always positive— some of it quite negative—but it's there and I think we have added to, and not taken from, our growth. When I say 'our,' I'm using that in a larger context. And I think that we have made a contribution in making this move. Many people tried to keep us out. You had your riots. But we made a tremendous contribution to the American growth, to the *American* development of *America*."

Among Lawrence's contemporaries, I can't think of anyone who combines a mastery of narrative with the mastery of the visual images. He has brought the two traditions together. "We are absolutely a people telling stories," he says. "It seems like we are born talking and telling people about it. This series came out of that—people talking about people coming up from the South. This tradition continues. 'Another family arrived. . . .' The train station—these images repeat themselves over and over again [in the series]—the share-cropper, the tenant farmer. This particular image—panel 31—represents my experience with the tenements. I think it's a very important work. The fire escape—in much of my work, I use [this] image, . . . which appears over and over again. If I had had the experience of seeing the fire escape and windows and tenements prior to [coming to Harlem], . . . I didn't realize it. But there was this visual image—a beautiful image—that occurred over and over again. I also want to say, by the ages of 14, 15, 16, I was making visits to the Metropolitan Museum of Art and . . . not trying to analyze it. Just going and looking and seeing and appreciating, especially the early Renaissance, and beginning to wonder how a person could put things down on a surface and make things seem to recede and seem to advance. It's like magic. . . . How could a person paint a violin case and you feel the grain coming out of that? They were masters. I would go in and marvel at these things. How do you make a thing seem to be round and have form? It was like magic to me."

For Lawrence, learning to "see" the Great Migration through the paintings of the European Renaissance masters is indicative of his idea of artistic influence, generally, and of the relation between white and black culture, specifically. "You're a part of us and we're a part of you," he says. Migration, in the end, fissured southern and northern black cultures into two distinct entities, as fundamentally related to their regions as to race. And because of Jacob Lawrence, the great narrative of a migrating, mutating culture is preserved forever on canvas, in sixty vividly sublime panels, a testament to a great historical epoch and to the vision of a modern master.

Jack Delano. Migratory workers on their way from Florida to New Jersey, 1940 (Library of Congress, Farm Security Administration Collection)

A Historian's Eye: Jacob Lawrence, Historical Reality, and the *Migration* Series

LONNIE G. BUNCH III AND SPENCER R. CREW

In the early twentieth century, most scholars ignored the contributions of African Americans to American history and culture. They saw only slave history, and they did not believe that people who were still adjusting to Western civilization could have a significant role in the American story. Moving against this current of thought were a small group whose research led them to black men and women whose contributions rivaled those of some of the most renowned politicians and scientists. Scholars such as George W. Williams, Carter G. Woodson, and Benjamin Brawley sought to explain the centrality of the African American experience to the evolution of the United States.[1] Not everyone interested in keeping this story alive was an academician like Woodson or Brawley. Additional "historians" came from other walks of life; their skills lay not in the crafting of scholarly publications but in the creation of literature, theater, dance, and art.

Jacob Lawrence was one of these "historians." He understood the intertwining of the African American and American experiences and explicitly presented it in his work. In his earlier series—the subjects of which were Frederick Douglass, Toussaint L'Ouverture, and Harriet Tubman—extensive research shaped his understanding of his subjects and undergirded his images. The *Migration* series, however, related his research to his own life. Lawrence was part of the migration experience, and in his paintings he revealed the significance of that exodus as well as the bittersweet nature of the African American struggle to survive in the United States.

Jacob Lawrence's life—from his birth in Atlantic City, New Jersey, the new home of many southern migrants—mirrored the pattern of many African American families during the early twentieth century. Disillusioned with their lives in the South, they made their way north by the hundreds of thousands with the advent of World War I, seeking better economic opportunities as well as improved political and social conditions. Access to jobs once unavailable to northern black workers made southern blacks willing to chance the risks involved in the move, and their children experienced both the benefits and the problems that resulted.[2]

Lawrence and other children of the migration spent many hours listening to their parents, relatives, and neighbors describe their lives in the South and their journey northward in stories that must have been both exciting and frightening. Although some of these tales may have been embellished, the reality of the system that white southerners had created to control African Americans was indeed grim.

The purpose of the system was to reduce African Americans to second-class citizenship by denying them basic constitutional rights. By 1915 southern states had created a variety of legal devices to keep blacks from the ballot box. The most famous was the "grandfather clause," first added to the Louisiana state constitution in 1898 to deny the vote to anyone whose grandparents had not been eligible to vote in that state in 1867—a group that included most potential African American voters. Once Louisiana's clause passed the scrutiny of the Supreme Court, which had ruled earlier that race could not be a criterion for excluding eligible voters, other southern states adopted it and similar indirect strategies. Poll taxes, for example, which forced voters to pay a fee in order to vote, effectively disenfranchised the poor. Literacy tests required potential voters to read and interpret a passage from the state constitution or another document to the satisfaction of local election officials. African Americans, no matter how highly educated, inevitably failed these tests,

Arthur Rothstein. Sharecropper plowing, Montgomery County, Alabama, 1937 (Library of Congress, Farm Security Administration Collection)

Marion Post Wolcott. Family picking peas, Flint River Farms, Georgia, late 1930s (Library of Congress, Farm Security Administration Collection)

while others with much less education passed easily.[3]

Just as limiting was the southern economic system. Most African Americans lived in rural areas and worked as farmers or farm laborers. Very few owned the land they cultivated. Instead, they toiled as tenant farmers or sharecroppers who rented land from large landowners in exchange for a share of the crop. The size of the landowner's share could be one-quarter of the crop or more, depending on what the renter contributed. Sharecroppers often purchased supplies on credit at the local store, which might belong to the same landowner. In a bad year, they might find themselves deeply in debt. Often settling one year's debt with the proceeds from the next, they were trapped in a cycle of indebtedness, dependence, and inability to attain economic stability.[4]

Local customs and laws discouraged protest against the injustices of the sharecropping system and governed the social setting. Under segregation or "Jim Crow" statutes, African Americans sat in separate seating areas in public places, drank at segregated water fountains, and rode in segregated train cars. Segregation also shaped the educational system. The schools available to African Americans received little money and few supplies. The teachers were dedicated but overworked, and children were discouraged from attending school beyond the sixth grade. Many landlords and some economically hard-pressed parents believed children had much more value as field workers than as students and pressured them to leave school.[5]

Defiance of discriminatory laws and customs could have dire consequences, ranging from arrest and time at a work farm or convict camp to violent retaliation on the part of the Ku Klux Klan and others who terrorized the African American community. Between 1900 and 1914 more than 1,100 African Americans were lynched in the United States, the vast majority of them in southern states.[6]

To ameliorate the impact of the caste system, African Americans had their own survival mechanisms: churches, fraternal organizations, masonic groups, and school activities. But even these organizations were not always enough to counteract the stress people felt, and many began to explore their options in other parts of the country. During World War I, when industrial production increased as the civilian labor supply shrank, factory owners looked to the South. They advertised in black newspapers and sent in labor recruiters. Black publications such as the *Chicago*

Dorothea Lange. Plantation owner, Clarksdale, Mississippi, 1936. Published in Edwin Rosskam and Richard Wright, *Twelve Million Black Voices*, 1941 (Library of Congress, Farm Security Administration Collection)

Defender, the *Pittsburgh Courier*, and the *Amsterdam News* ran regular articles highlighting the advantages of living in the North and the problems confronting African Americans who remained in the South.

It has been argued that the Great Migration had its start when the Pennsylvania Railroad sent an employee south to recruit African American workers. His success encouraged others and unleashed the torrent of migration.[7] Indeed, the Pennsylvania Railroad eventually became one of the primary transporters of migrants to the Midatlantic and Northeast regions. Many of the newcomers, including the parents of Jacob Lawrence, settled in Atlantic City, a seaside resort where the demand for service workers was high.

In his *Migration* series Lawrence poignantly captured the heroism and the pathos that characterized black life in the South before and during the mass exodus northward. His aim was not to romanticize that life but to set forth clearly the conditions under which his parents, their relatives, and their neighbors had to live. He allowed these people, who had few avenues for voicing their experiences, to speak to the public that views the images. He listened closely to the stories of the people depicted in his paintings, and he wants the viewer to understand what these people endured.

A difficult and sometimes bleak existence comes through in Lawrence's images. The people portrayed are locked in a mighty struggle against poverty, nature, spiritual degradation, and physical violence, weights heavy enough to break anyone's spirit and perseverance. But the people Lawrence depicts not only survive their condition; they strike back at it by voting with their feet. Relocating was a conscious step to escape the system of repression erected in the South, a quiet rebellion against a system the migrants could not yet defeat but would not willingly or passively embrace.[8]

To African Americans whose roots reached back into the South or who still lived there, Lawrence's images told a painfully familiar story; for others, particularly those living outside of the South, they offered a glimpse into a totally new world. The *Migration* series removed the cloak of anonymity from a central element of the twentieth-century African American experience. It allowed the uninitiated to understand the toll southern racism took on its victims, the resiliency of African Americans, and the reasons so many people joined the stream of black workers heading north.[9] The series also portrayed African Americans as people who made deliberate choices about how to counteract the forces arrayed against them.

Of all the choices African Americans could make, migrating offered the most rapid opportunity to change their destinies. But what they found did not always match their expectations.

In the panels of the *Migration* series that focus on the northern experience, Lawrence continued his depiction of a determined, proud people willing to sacrifice to ensure a better life for future generations. Yet his complex narrative does not romanticize the massive transition from rural South to urban North. One of his strengths is his ability to struggle with and convey to his audiences—knowledgeable and uninitiated alike—the complexities, ambiguities, expectations, and disappointments that shaped the African American condition during this time. He understood that just as slavery had shaped African American life in the nineteenth century, migration would become the defining event of the twentieth.

Lawrence was one of many who clarified and defined the migration experience; from the end of World War I through the early stages of World War II, the story of the migration was like an omnipresent hum heard everywhere blacks settled. While much of what Lawrence knew of it came from his research or from his family and friends, his vision may also have been shaped by the cultural milieu of black centers such as Harlem, where the newcomers' hopes informed much of the era's literature, music, and even the nascent black theater and film. Lawrence's art expressed both the unschooled and unstructured memories of the migrants and the creative and intellectual products of the literati, actors, and musicians of the cultural movements of the 1920s (the Harlem Renaissance) and the 1930s and 1940s (the New Realism).[10]

In any newly created black metropolis of this period, a complex atmosphere influenced cultural life. The arduous trip, the difficult change in surroundings, the struggle to remain connected to family and friends "down South," and the migrants' shifting expectations all contributed to the black urban experience. Some of the writers, especially

during the early 1920s, were overly optimistic. To them, coming north meant not only a rejection of southern bigotry and violence but an opportunity to reap the full benefits of American democracy in an environment shaped by and conducive to African Americans.

Thus Claude McKay spoke of finally coming "Home to Harlem" after a life of wandering, while James Weldon Johnson wrote that the vibrancy and strength of black Harlem was "a miracle straight out of the skies." To Johnson, the unprecedented opportunities that the North provided would allow blacks to forever end the notion of being "beggar[s] at the gates of the nation waiting to be thrown the crumbs of civilization." Langston Hughes, who celebrated and romanticized the rhythms and possibilities of the city, was overwhelmed with optimism: "I went up the steps [of the subway] and out into the bright September sunlight. Harlem! I stood there, dropped my bags, took a deep breath and felt happy again." Rudolph Fisher, a keen and critical observer of urban black life, explored the inflated expectation that migration would bring freedom, money, and refuge. In his short story, "The City of Refuge," Fisher wrote: "In Harlem, black was white. You had rights that could not be denied you; you had privileges, protected by law. And you had money. It was a land of plenty." Artists such as Archibald Motley and singers such as Ethel Waters, in their rush to embrace the possibilities of urbanization, often understated or overlooked the harsher realities.[11]

By the end of the Harlem Renaissance, writers, poets, and musicians had begun to document the impact of overcrowding, the resiliency of racism in the North, the ravages of disease, and the limited share of the economic pie. They began to reflect the prevailing wisdom that for the migrants, the city "ain't been no crystal stair."[12] Much of the music of the 1930s also reflected this approach. In the musical suite, "Black, Brown and Beige," Duke Ellington realistically depicted "many aspects of the city within a city—good and bad." Bessie Smith's "Backwater Blues" encouraged the movement north but also cautioned that it would not guarantee an escape from the blues; Mead Lux Lewis's "Honky Tonk Train Blues" captured the feel of the trains that brought migrants north and the subways that confined and shook their tenements each night.[13]

Black authors of the period wrestled with the unfulfilled hopes of migration. Searching for greater reality, they replaced the cabaret of the Harlem Renaissance with the tenement. Jean Toomer's celebrated novel *Cane* explored the ugliness of race relations in the South as well as the impact of the city on black lives and aspirations. Ultimately, he suggested, there was no racial panacea in either the city or the country. Even Langston Hughes's poetry began to reflect the realization that change did not come simply by the act of moving north and congregating in black enclaves. In "Elevator Boy" he wrote: "I got a job now/ running an elevator/ in the Dennison Hotel in Jersey/ Job ain't no good though/ no money around."[14] William Attaway's novel *Blood on the Forge* (1941) was critical of those who celebrated factory work as heroic; the migrants, he argued, were exchanging familiar southern violence for the strange and savage violence of the northern factories. But the most critical examination of migration was Richard Wright's novel *Native Son* (1941). The tragedy that befell the protagonist, Bigger Thomas, had much to do with poverty, racism, and the clash between the migrant's expectations and the reality of urban life.[15]

From the art, music, and literature of his day, Jacob Lawrence assimilated this dizzying array of messages and viewpoints. His *Migration* series reflects a sophisticated melding of optimistic, romantic notions of the city with a more pessimistic, darker evaluation of urbanization. Lawrence's ability to marry memory, scholarship, popular culture, and a historian's eye ensured that the series would transcend caricature and simplistic assessment to stand as an artistic creation rich with historical detail and ripe with the complexities and nuances that shaped and informed the Great Migration. Lawrence accomplished something that would have been difficult for an academically trained historian to achieve: he crafted a narrative that was built on historical reality and embraced the ambiguities of the past, and then he made that narrative teach, entertain, and sing.

The urban moments in Lawrence's *Migration* series make it clear that he sought to reflect the ambivalence of black life in the North. His images suggest the tensions between expectations and disappointments, between what was gained and what was lost. But above all, they suggest the often

Dorothea Lange. Workers hoeing in field, Georgia, ca. 1941. Published in Edwin Rosskam and Richard Wright, *Twelve Million Black Voices*, 1941, and selected by The Museum of Modern Art for the title panel of its installation of the *Migration* series in 1944 (Library of Congress, Farm Security Administration Collection)

harsh realities that the migrants experienced. Yet "the migrants kept coming."

For many migrants the first reality of urban life involved finding a place to live. While black communities accommodated the first trickle of the movement, later migrants found their housing opportunities limited by custom, cost, and rapidly diminishing availability. White political and community leaders worked to restrict the newcomers to existing black neighborhoods. All those who migrated to Pittsburgh, for example, were shunted into the Hill District, those in Los Angeles were relegated to the Central Avenue corridor, and those in New York found Harlem home. Municipalities enforced this arrangement either through intimidation or through legal arrangements such as residential housing covenants that restricted home ownership to white people. The quality of housing declined in black areas, as houses and apartments were subdivided into overcrowded, smaller living spaces. Disease, poverty, and crime began to take their toll; in black Harlem, for example, the tuberculosis rate was the highest in the city.[16]

Racial discrimination in all aspects of life was as much a part of the northern experience as it was in the South. While the blatant signs of the South were not a part of the northern landscape, Jim Crow was alive and roaming the streets. Restaurants, hotels, residential communities, businesses, and schools restricted access based more on custom than on law. In the cities the separation of the races was even more extreme than in the South.

Exerting their rights as citizens, blacks often tried to change or circumvent these discriminatory customs, only to find their attempts thwarted by their lack of political or economic clout. Occasionally the increased black presence and the pressure for change sparked violence, as Jacob Lawrence shows in panel 52 of the *Migration* series depicting the 1919 East St. Louis riot. In fact, many scholars argue that the Harlem riot in 1935 ended any notion that the city offered a panacea for African Americans.[17]

Just as limiting was discrimination in employment. Manpower shortages caused first by World War I and later by the restructuring of immigration policy gave African Americans their entrée to northern factories, yet they were relegated to unskilled or semiskilled positions, due in part to the reluctance of unions to accept them as members. Black workers were also used as strikebreakers in labor conflicts that sometimes turned violent, and the violence often was directed at the city's black enclave. Studies of major urban

Jack Delano. At the bus station, 1940 (Library of Congress, Farm Security Administration Collection)

centers in the 1920s, 1930s, and 1940s indicate that black employment was still mostly limited to the lowest-paying unskilled or service sectors. The migrants struggled, much as they had in the South, to provide for their families.

Despite the many disappointments, the movement north did offer opportunities that made the transition worth the effort. An important attraction was the right to vote, which, while it did not ameliorate all the ills that the migrants faced, nonetheless provided a limited chance to exert modest political influence. Although white politicians used a variety of means, including gerrymandering, to limit the impact of the black vote, soon the black communities gained political power sheerly by virtue of their size. By the time Lawrence painted the *Migration* series, there were a growing number of local black politicians and even a few black members of the House of Representatives, including Oscar DePriest of Chicago and Adam Clayton Powell of Harlem.

The migration also brought the need and the opportunity for new churches and community organizations to help the settlers find employment, housing, medical treatment, educational facilities, and relatives or friends. These groups smoothed the transition to an alien environment that often invalidated the migrants' traditions, practices, and frames of reference.[18]

As Lawrence wrote in his narrative, many earlier African American migrants to northern cities "met their fellowmen with disgust and aloofness" (panel 53), an attitude that grew out of class and regional differences. Many in the established black community feared that the new migrants might, with their uncouth ways and southernism, undermine their own tenuous status. While these concerns were understandable, they created divisions that inhibited cohesiveness at a time when a united front in the various African American communities might have elevated them more quickly.

While the *Migration* series was a brilliant vehicle for giving voice to part of the American population that had long been a shadowy presence, its public showing in 1941 and subsequent tour beginning in 1942 also offered contemporary lessons to African Americans. Here they saw depicted the hopes and dreams of an earlier generation that had headed north seeking fuller participation as citizens. That generation also listened to W.E.B. Du Bois, editor of *The Crisis*, who counseled African Americans to "Close Ranks" and forgo their quest for greater equality in order to join

Arthur Rothstein. Tenement section, Pittsburgh, Pennsylvania, 1941. Published in Edwin Rosskam and Richard Wright, *Twelve Million Black Voices*, 1941 (Library of Congress, Farm Security Administration Collection)

their countrymen in the fight against tyranny during World War I.[19] Their response was to sue for the right to participate in the military draft. That generation set aside personal concerns and worked in war industries, only to lose their jobs when white soldiers returned. And they fought gallantly and died for their country in segregated units, only to return to race riots, lynching, and limited economic opportunity. Hoping that by displaying their patriotism they would prove their worthiness for full economic and political recognition, they came home to face greater restrictions and determined opposition to their efforts.[20]

As Lawrence's *Migration* series appeared on the national scene, once again African Americans seeking better lives were leaving the South and moving to cities in the West, Midwest, and East. Once again the demands of a world war were opening new job alternatives and offering the opportunity to press for better treatment of all citizens. African Americans who saw the series in the early 1940s must have thought about the lessons of that earlier movement and about how they might avoid the same bitter disappointments.

Leaders like A. Philip Randolph and Bayard Rustin contemplated past disappointments and created the March on Washington Movement. To protest job discrimination by companies that received government contracts, they planned a march on Washington, D.C., unless President Franklin D. Roosevelt sponsored legislation prohibiting such practices. They knew that a mass protest would embarrass the government, which was fighting a war to preserve democracy in other parts of the world.

Other leaders adopted a different attitude toward African American participation in World War II. They called for a two-front war, one outside the nation's boundaries and the other within, where racism and discrimination still had a firm hold. These leaders were unwilling to return to business as usual. They were determined to use this migration and

this war as a springboard to improve the status of African Americans.[21]

Not everyone who viewed Lawrence's *Migration* series during its debut and tour saw the lessons it contained, but the similarities between its images and the historical events of that moment were self-evident. As Lawrence has said, his works are portraits of himself, his family, and his peers—they are a part of him.[22] And this series in particular is very much a part of the African American community. It reveals accepted communal truths to African Americans while making these truths available to others in a manner that challenges, provokes, and educates. In essence, the *Migration* series successfully captures the feel, the tensions, and the historical events that shaped and accompanied the massive movement of rural blacks to northern cities. Created at the dawn of World War II, it also documents the strengths, ambiguities, and dilemmas that shaped the northern African American community as it stood on the threshold of fundamental change.

John Vachon. Courtroom scene, Virginia, ca. 1941. Published in Edwin Rosskam and Richard Wright, *Twelve Million Black Voices,* 1941 (Library of Congress, Farm Security Administration Collection)

NOTES

1. Williams, *History of the Negro Race* (New York: G. P. Putnam's Sons, 1883); Woodson, *The Negro in Our History* (Washington, D.C.: Association for Study of Negro Life and Culture, 1922); Brawley, *A Short History of the American Negro,* (1919; New York: Macmillan, 1950).

2. Lerone Bennett, Jr., *Confrontation: Black and White* (Baltimore: Penguin Books, 1965), 114–15.

3. C. Vann Woodward, *Origins of the New South 1877–1913* (Baton Rouge: Louisiana State University Press, 1951), 321–49.

4. Emmett J. Scott, *Negro Migration During the War* (1920; New York: Arno Press, 1969), 14–17.

5. Bennett, *Confrontation,* 78–83; Benjamin Quarles, *The Negro in the Making of America* (New York: Collier Macmillan, 1969), 144–47.

6. John Hope Franklin, *From Slavery to Freedom: A History of Negro Americans* (New York: Alfred A. Knopf, 1974), 322–23.

7. Charles A. Hardy III, "Race and Opportunity: Black Philadelphia During the Era of the Great Migration" (Ph.D. diss., Temple University, 1989), 118; Scott, *Negro Migration,* 54–55.

8. Bennett, *Confrontation,* 115.

9. ". . . And the Migrants Kept Coming," *Fortune* 24, no. 5 (November 1941): 102.

10. For an excellent discussion of the intersection between cultural creativity and the new black enclaves of the 1920s and 1930s, see Cary Wintz, *Black Culture and the Harlem Renaissance* (Houston: Rice University Press, 1988) and Nathan Huggins, *The Harlem Renaissance* (New York: Oxford University Press, 1976).

11. Robert Bone, *The Negro Novel in America* (New Haven: Yale University Press, 1968), 74–78; Wintz, *Black Culture,* 82–84; and Alain Locke, ed., *The New Negro* (1925; New York: Atheneum, 1968), 58.

12. Langston Hughes, "Mother to Son," in *Selected Poems of Langston Hughes* (New York: Vintage Books, 1974), 187.

13. Stanley Dance, liner notes to Duke Ellington, "Black, Brown and Beige"

Photographer unknown. Children playing in Harlem, 1930s (National Archives)

(Washington, D.C.: Smithsonian Recordings, 1989); Marshall W. Stearns, *The Story of Jazz* (New York: Oxford University Press, 1956), 168–71.

14. Quoted in Wintz, *Black Culture*, 84–85.

15. Bone *Negro Novel*, 140–44.

16. The study of African American migration is now one of the most active fields of historical scholarship. Among the best of this genre are Joe Trotter, *Black Milwaukee: The Making of an Industrial Proletariat* (Urbana: University of Illinois Press, 1985) and Jervis Anderson, *This Was Harlem* (New York: Farrar, Straus & Giroux, 1981). Much of this discussion of Harlem is indebted to Wintz, *Black Culture*, 5–36.

17. See Wintz, *Black Culture*, 12–20, and Gilbert Osofsky, *Harlem: The Making of a Ghetto* (New York: Harper and Row, 1964).

18. For a discussion of the array of community organizations that grew out of these new black communities, see Lonnie G. Bunch, *Black Angelenos: The African American in Los Angeles* (Los Angeles: California Afro-American Museum, 1988), 27–32.

19. W.E.B. Du Bois, "Close Ranks," *The Crisis* 16 (July 1918): 110–16.

20. Franklin, *From Slavery to Freedom*, 353–67.

21. Benjamin Quarles, *The Negro in the Making of America*, 215–16.

22. Jacob Lawrence, interview with Elizabeth Hutton Turner, Seattle, Washington, October 3, 1992.

Researchers in the Division of Negro History, Literature, and Prints, 135th Street Branch Library (now known as the Schomburg Center for Research in Black Culture), 1930s (National Archives, Harmon Foundation Collection)

The Schomburg Collection:
A Rich Resource for Jacob Lawrence

DEBORAH WILLIS

What impresses me about Lawrence is his ability to combine social interest and interpretation (he selects his own episodes from careful library reading and research) with a straight art approach when he comes to work on his drawings.[1]

—Alain Le Roy Locke

Few modern paintings can claim their origins in a library. But before Jacob Lawrence ever picked up his brush, he often went to the library and researched or wrote the text for the story he was about to tell. To an artist like Lawrence, a library is the soul of history; its resources are like sketches for undeveloped ideas. Lawrence the storyteller used the library to interpret, study, and create works about particular historical or contemporary events. The Schomburg Collection of Negro History, Literature, and Prints, in a branch of the New York Public Library in Harlem, played a strong supporting role in creating the realist themes found in his paintings.

Housed in a McKim, Mead, and White structure on West 135th Street, the branch library gave the young Lawrence access to a vast body of information. The Schomburg Collection, now known as the Schomburg Center for Research in Black Culture, is one of the most renowned research centers shaped by and devoted to the activities and achievements of Africans and Africans in the diaspora. Many artists and scholars—among them Langston Hughes and James Weldon Johnson—have found the collection to be both a rich intellectual resource and a powerful creative and spiritual stimulus.

When the 135th Street Branch Library opened on January 14, 1905, turn-of-the-century Harlem was growing and changing rapidly. It was a blend of white working-class neighborhoods whose residents were of European origin and, especially west of Lenox Avenue, one of the largest upper-middle-class enclaves in Manhattan.[2] By 1919 a new migration had occurred as black southerners moved north to the cities, and the Harlem community presented a decidedly different picture. Ernestine Rose, who was appointed librarian of the 135th Street Branch in 1920, observed the same year that the elementary school opposite the library had an enrollment of more than 2,000 children, 90 percent of whom were "colored," and that there were eight "colored" teachers. Most likely in response to this influx of "colored" students, the school's principal suggested to Rose that "colored help would be [an] advantage to the work of the branch library."[3] Shortly thereafter, the New York Public

James Van Der Zee. *Chocolate Soda Wagon*, in front of 135th Street Branch Library, 1928 (copyright 1969 James Van Der Zee, all rights reserved, courtesy of Donna Mussenden-Van Der Zee)

Aaron Douglas and Arthur Schomburg at the 135th Street Branch Library, ca. 1934, viewing the 1934 mural by Douglas, *Aspects of Negro Life: Song of the Towers* (National Archives, Harmon Foundation Collection)

Library hired its first black librarian, Catherine Allen Latimer, and assigned her to the 135th Street Branch.

In May 1925 the branch inaugurated the Division of Negro History, Literature, and Prints "to preserve the historical record of the race; to arouse the race consciousness and race pride; to inspire art students [and] to give information to everyone about the Negro."[4] Celeste Tibbets describes the urgency that Ernestine Rose felt: "Questions of identity and heritage were pressing; artists and writers framed these questions articulately for the populace and found a home in the 135th Street Library."[5] Jean Blackwell Hutson, curator of the Schomburg Collection from 1948 to 1980, observed that Harlem residents had such a "relentless intellectual thirst" for black and African history that "rare and out-of-print books could not be replaced when they were 'worn to

shreds,' and books still in print could not be replaced fast enough with the money available."[6]

Mindful of the challenge to quench this thirst and create a library devoted to community needs, Rose invited Arthur A. Schomburg, a bibliophile and a Puerto Rican of African ancestry, to chair a committee charged with planning for the preservation of the heavily used collection.[7] Schomburg loaned a portion of his large private collection of black history material to the library, and others joined in the effort: scholar Hubert Harrison organized weekly lectures on black history, while Catherine Latimer established a clippings file and a small collection of books on the subject.[8] The committee assessed the condition of the circulating books and separated those that were considered rare. The committee and library staff urged members of the community to donate or loan books, journals, artworks, and photographs.

Rose knew that Schomburg was interested in selling his collection. She wrote to L. Hollingsworth Wood, president of the National Urban League, seeking his support for bringing the collection to the 135th Street Branch:

> Mr. Schomburg . . . has loaned some of his books, and I have learned that his collection is for sale. . . . I learned now that Mr. George Foster Peabody is considering the purchase of this collection with a view to giving it to a university in Africa.
>
> I can see the suitability of this from some standpoints, but I feel with many others that it would be a calamity to let this collection leave the United States, where it should serve the purpose of enlightenment to both races and where such an educational process is so necessary.[9]

Schomburg met with Wood and members of his staff to discuss a suitable repository for his collection. The obvious choice was the 135th Street Branch. The New York Public Library received a $10,000 grant from the Carnegie Corporation to purchase the collection. On January 20, 1927, the Arthur A. Schomburg Collection officially opened on the third floor of the branch.

The collection that inspired Jacob Lawrence has never been a traditional library. It has always served the community in diverse ways. Ernestine Rose described its impact in an annual report for the 135th Street Branch from about 1936:

I have endeavored to make the [Schomburg] collection . . . available to readers, students and scholars. . . . The periodical and magazine files are used by a goodly number of persons who keep in touch with the chronicled events of their respective sectional parts of the country. We can mention a number of books written by scholars where expressions of acknowledgment have been given, such as in Prof. Loggins' book, "Negro Author"; the poet, James Weldon Johnson's "Black Manhattan"; Nancy Cunard, in her book "Negro Anthology"; and many others. Their works were primarily based on the books they found on our shelves.[10]

In addition to books, manuscripts, and maps, the collection included two- and three-dimensional artworks. The library had large exhibit cases and a theater where plays and poetry readings were staged. The Harlem Art Workshop, where Jacob Lawrence first studied as a youngster, held its classes in the basement. In the mid-1930s, Roberta Bosely, one of the newly hired black librarians, hung an early drawing by young Jacob Lawrence in an exhibition. After he saw the drawing, Carter G. Woodson, historian and founder of the Association of Negro Life and History and author of the definitive study on the Great Migration, remarked that Lawrence was not talented enough to become a successful artist.[11] The library also collected published materials from the local school district. One of Lawrence's poems, "To all mothers," published in the December 1930 *P.S. 89 Parent-Teacher Bulletin*, is still preserved in the library's vast collection.

Even during the Great Depression, Harlem was a colorful and expressive place. Lawrence recalls that he walked the avenues and streets recording people and events in his memory in an attempt to learn about and understand the history of black people. The library offered many programs and lectures on black history for community groups.[12] Lawrence attended these meetings, which were led by community historians in the library and the local YMCA, and listened intently to the street-corner orators.

The tradition of the street-corner orator in Harlem had its roots as early as 1915. These speakers, who attracted large and enthusiastic audiences, suggested to Ernestine Rose a way for the 135th Street Branch to bring people to the library:

It occurred to us that if people will listen to politics and patent medicines they will listen to education, too, provided it is well presented to them. So we employed one of the most eloquent and the most popular of these speakers and paid him to address large crowds at strategic corners on the streets of Harlem. Once a week these people were urged to come to a meeting at the library. This was one of our most successful attempts to reach the "common man."[13]

Augusta Baker, a librarian who began her career at the 135th Street Branch, recalled:

The basic training was that we were a part of the community. We were not to sit inside and wait for people to come to us. We were to go out to them and invite them in. We were to make the Branch so inviting that they would want to come back."[14]

A report published in 1940 clearly shows that the Schomburg was serving the needs of a diverse community. From August through November 1939, 3,359 people used the collection; two thematic exhibitions—on African art from Nigeria and photographs and books from the Virgin

Jack Allison. Utopia Children's House, Harlem, summer 1938 (Library of Congress, Farm Security Administration Collection)

Islands—were on display. Recognizing the changing needs of the community, the librarians began to record new and unusual reference questions.

In 1940 and 1941 they responded to queries dealing with issues as varied as "stories behind the spirituals"; "poems on Haiti by Negro poets"; "social conditions of Negroes during the slavery period"; the Negro in the field of baseball"; and "Negro Baptists in Pennsylvania." Librarian Catherine Latimer noted in a report on reference work that bibliographies were developed as a direct result of users' questions on "Harlem," "the Negro in agriculture," and "outstanding Negro men and women of New York who have helped the Negro in all fields and periods of American History." A year-long exhibition, "The Birth of a Book," displayed manuscripts by Langston Hughes, Charles S. Johnson, Melville Herskovits, Countee Cullen, W.E.B. Du Bois, W. C. Handy, Henrietta Buckmaster, Richard Wright, and others.[15]

In 1939 the noted historian Lawrence D. Reddick succeeded Arthur A. Schomburg as curator of the collection. Following a survey to assess the needs of scholars and community residents, the collection expanded its holdings by acquiring a range of newspapers, books, and magazines, accommodating the newly arrived migrants.

By 1941 the Schomburg provided a wealth of resources for Jacob Lawrence's inquiry into the Great Migration. Sixteen years after the collection was established, it offered lecture series, art and drama workshops, and the core library material— manuscripts, periodicals, works of art, and archival collections. Ernestine Rose wrote that "the function of a library in any community is to act as a natural center for the development of the community's intellectual life; it will be the library's duty and privilege to search out and encourage any activity which quickens . . . aesthetic interest."[16] Inspired by this thinking, Lawrence engulfed himself in his subject by searching through books, newspapers, magazines, prints, and photographs. Sometimes serendipitously, but most often methodically and deliberately, he looked for source material to illustrate his ideas. Like the poet and novelist Langston Hughes before him, he made the 135th Street Branch Library his first stop. He created the framework for his stories using the histories and statistics housed there.

Access to the Schomburg Collection was through a row of card catalogue drawers. Seeking material on the subject of

the Great Migration, Lawrence browsed the catalogue looking for references for his new series. In his 1940 application for a fellowship from the Julius Rosenwald Fund, he described his plan of work: "Most of my research (about 6 months work) would be carried on at the Negro History division of the Schomburg Library."[16]

Lawrence divided his proposal into eight sections, each posing a focused question on the issue of migration. Looking in the card catalogue in 1940 under the subject heading "Migration, Negro: see Negroes—Migration," he would have found a large and comprehensive collection. Although he does not cite specific texts, he might have selected books and essays with titles such as *The Negro Question in the United States*, by James Stewart Allen (1936); *The Northward Movement of the Colored Population*, by Frederick J. Brown (ca. 1897); *Factors in Cultural Backgrounds of the British West Indian Negro and the American Southern Negro that Condition Their Adjustments in Harlem*, by Barrington Dunbar (1936); *Negro Migration: A Study of the Exodus of the Negroes 1920 and 1925 from Middle Georgia Counties as that Exodus Was Influenced or Determined by Existing Economic Conditions*, by John William Fanning (1930); "Conditions Among Negroes in the Cities," by George Edmund Haynes, published in the *Bulletin of the National League on Urban Conditions Among Negroes* (1913); *The*

Jacob Lawrence (second from left) making block prints under the direction of Sarah West at a WPA Federal Art Project workshop, Harlem, ca. 1933–34 (National Archives, Harmon Foundation Collection)

Jacob Lawrence (center) and other students with their teacher at a WPA Federal Art Project workshop, Harlem, ca. 1933–34 (National Archives, Harmon Foundation Collection)

Negro Peasant Turns Cityward: Effects of Recent Migrations to North Centers, by Louise Veneable Kennedy (1930); *Negro Intelligence and Selective Migration*, by Otto Klineberg; and *Negro Migration During the War*, by Emmett Jay Scott (1920). Other valuable references on the subject that could have aroused Lawrence's interest were Alain Locke's *The New Negro: An Interpretation* (1925) and the research files of the Writers' Program of the Work Projects Administration, *Negroes of New York* (1939–40).

The clippings maintained by librarian Catherine Latimer contained crucial and interesting visual references. It is ironic, however, that while Lawrence studied the printed word for relevance and authenticity, he says he does not recall using the extensive photographic files in the collection to stimulate his imagination for the *Migration* series. The Resettlement Administration (later the Farm Security Administration) Photographic File had a large collection of photographs of migrant workers and southern scenes. Studio portraits, snapshots, and street portraits of Harlem families

were also a part of the library's photographic files as early as the late 1920s. Most of this material was located in the general research collection. Nor does Lawrence cite specific texts as sources.

Lawrence's research methods for the *Migration* series probably paralleled those he used for his first narrative cycle, forty-one paintings on the Haitian leader Toussaint L'Ouverture (1937–38). Inspired first by the W.E.B. Du Bois play *Haiti* at the Lafayette Theater in 1936, he began reading about L'Ouverture and the history of the Republic of Haiti:

I do my research first; read the books, take notes. I may find it necessary to go through my notes three times to eliminate unimportant points. I did all my reading at [the] Schomburg Library. Most of the information came from Charles Beard's book *Toussaint L'Ouverture*. I read other books—there were more novels than anything else. One book, I don't remember its name, told me of the conditions on the island and its resources. It gave a short sketch of the history of the Haitian revolution.[18]

Jacob Lawrence. *The Curator*, 1937, gouache on paper (Art and Artifacts Division, Schomburg Center for Research in Black Culture, The New York Public Library, Astor, Lenox, and Tilden Foundations)

Lawrence used the same method with his series on Frederick Douglass (1938–39) and Harriet Tubman (1939–40).

The Schomburg also inspired other works by Lawrence. In 1937, just one year before the untimely death of Arthur A. Schomburg, he executed a gouache on paper called *The Curator*, which is now in the Schomburg Center collection. In a 1977 letter to Jean Blackwell Hutson, he wrote:

> The painting is not an exact portrait painting of Arthur Schomburg, however, many years ago I spent much of my time at the Schomburg Collection and the library did inspire me to paint this picture. I am very pleased it is now part of the Center's permanent collection.[19]

Lawrence clearly believed that "history paintings" should be based on actual recorded events. At the Schomburg, where art was displayed with books, he found the courage to make his story into an aesthetic statement. The Schomburg—forged during the migration—fit the very nature of the story Lawrence wanted to tell. As Langston Hughes described it, the collection was both the well that drew the intelligentsia and the hub of the spinning wheel of ideas that sent them out again. In his essay, "My Early Days in Harlem," Hughes described his first visit to the 135th Street Library in 1921:

> [A] warm and wonderful librarian, Miss Ernestine Rose, white, made newcomers feel welcome, as did her assistant in charge of the Schomburg Collection, Catherine Latimer, a luscious café au lait.[20]

Hughes went on to evoke the Harlem of the migration:

> Harlem, like a Picasso painting in his cubistic period. Harlem—Southern Harlem—the Carolinas, Georgia, Florida—looking for the Promised Land—dressed in rhythmic words, painted in bright pictures, dancing to jazz—and ending up in the subway at morning rush time—headed downtown. West Indian Harlem—warm rambunctious sassy remembering Marcus Garvey. Haitian Harlem, Cuban Harlem, little pockets of tropical dreams in alien tongues. Magnet Harlem, pulling an Arthur Schomburg from Puerto Rico, pulling an Arna Bontemps all the way from California, a Nora Holt from way out West, an E. Simms Campbell from St. Louis, likewise a Josephine Baker, a Charles S. Johnson from Virginia, an A. Philip Randolph from Florida, a Roy Wilkins from Minnesota, an Alta Douglas from Kansas. Melting pot Harlem—Harlem of honey and chocolate and caramel and rum and vinegar and lemon and lime and gall.[21]

The pulse of Hughes's essay reflects the sentiments and ideas that influenced Lawrence's paintings of Harlem and its people. The Schomburg Collection was a creative partner to the artist as he constructed and forged his *Migration* series. In the Schomburg, he found his greatest inspiration and his greatest sanctuary.

NOTES

1. Alain Locke to Julius Rosenwald Fund, "Confidential Report on Candidate for Fellowship," re Jacob Armstead Lawrence, January 23, 1940, Rosenwald Fund Collection, Special Collections, Fisk University, Nashville, Tenn. (hereafter Rosenwald Fund Collection).

2. Jervis Anderson, *This Was Harlem: 1900–1950* (New York: Farrar, Straus, and Giroux, 1981), 45.

3. Quoted in Elinor Des Verney Sinnette, *Arthur A. Schomburg: Black Bibliophile and Collector, A Biography* (Detroit: New York Public Library and Wayne State University Press, 1989), 131.

4. Ibid., 132.

5. Celeste Tibbets, *Ernestine Rose and the Origins of the Schomburg Center*, Schomburg Center Occasional Papers Series, no. 2 (New York: New York Public Library, 1989), 21.

6. Jean Blackwell Hutson, "The Schomburg Collection," *Freedomways*, Summer 1963, 432.

7. Arthur Alphonso Schomburg (1874–1938) had a lifelong passion for collecting, which reportedly sprang from a childhood experience when a grammar school teacher responded to his question about black history by informing him that black people had no history. Among the other community members of the planning committee were writer James Weldon Johnson, real estate investor John A. Nail, and scholar and lecturer Hubert Harrison.

8. Sinnette, *Schomburg*, 132.

9. Ernestine Rose to L. Hollingsworth Wood, October 6, 1925, Rare Books, Manuscripts, and Archives Division, Schomburg Center Records, Schomburg Center for Research in Black Culture, New York Public Library (hereafter Schomburg Center Records).

10. Ernestine Rose, "Annual Report," n.d. (ca. 1936), 1, Schomburg Center Records.

11. Sinnette, *Schomburg*, 224.

12. Tibbets, *Rose*, 25.

13. Ibid. Originally quoted in Margaret E. Monroe, *Library Adult Education: The Biography of an Idea* (New York: Scarecrow Press, 1963), 311–12.

14. Tibbets, *Rose*, 23.

15. Catherine A. Latimer, "Report of Reference Work in Schomburg Collection, 1941" (submitted December 16, 1941), 2, Schomburg Center Records.

16. Sinnette, *Schomburg*, 135.

17. Jacob Lawrence, fellowship application submitted to Julius Rosenwald Fund, 1940, Rosenwald Fund Collection.

18. Press release, "Life of Toussaint L'Ouverture," by Jacob Lawrence, exhibition held at De Porres Interracial Center, New York, May 22–June 2, 1939, 2, Manuscript Division, Library of Congress.

19. Jacob Lawrence to Jean Blackwell Hutson, June 28, 1977. Art and Artifacts Division, Schomburg Center for Research in Black Culture, New York Public Library.

20. Langston Hughes and John Henrik Clark, eds., *Harlem: A Community in Transition* (New York: Citadel Press, 1964), 62.

21. Ibid., 64.

Carl Van Vechten. *Alain Locke*, 1941 (National Portrait Gallery, Smithsonian Institution, copyright estate of Carl Van Vechten, Joseph Solomon, executor)

(Un)Locke(ing) Jacob Lawrence's Migration Series

JEFFREY C. STEWART

With engaging, disarming frankness, Jacob Lawrence graciously welcomed the questions of historians, art critics, and museum professionals during preparations for The Phillips Collection's exhibition of his *Migration* series: Did he study Mexican muralists? Was he affected by the work of the Black photographer James Van Der Zee? Had he ever met Alfred Stieglitz? Had he been part of the celebrated debate between Richard Wright and Zora Neale Hurston over the effects of racism and folk traditions on the psychology of African Americans?[1]

Just as graciously, Lawrence dismissed these inquiries as largely irrelevant to his artistic vision. His sources, he said again and again, were his community. His Harlem schoolteachers had recognized early his special gift and encouraged his artistic talent. His visits to the Apollo Theater on 135th Street had opened his eyes to the theater; coming out of that palace of African American dance and vaudeville, he had made boxes into little stages on which he mounted his first artistic compositions. He drew his inspiration from the streets around him, a kind of theater in its own right, with a range of personalities from barefoot prophets to shell-shocked World War I veterans, from street-corner Garveyites who advocated return to Africa to soapbox Communists who predicted the worldwide triumph of an integrated proletariat—all clamoring, all gesturing, all transforming a northern ghetto into a creative crucible called Harlem. That was the laboratory of Lawrence's artistic genius, along with the interiors of Black homes that had been fancy upper-middle-class apartments but by the 1930s were worn and tattered tenements groaning under the weight of successive waves of migrants whose lives Lawrence's series chronicled. Those tenements, with their brightly decorated interiors and garish facades, had been the educators of his eye.

Lawrence was telling us that he and other African American and European American artists—Aaron Douglas and Stuart Davis, for instance—were inspired more by the community of Harlem than by each other. Not just on a social but also on a formal level, Black urban communities like Harlem were kaleidoscopes of pattern, color, movement, and design that the awakened eye—and there were precious few of them—could distill and transform into a tapestry that came to define an African American aesthetic in the visual arts. Lawrence knew not only the aesthetic form of his community but also the content of the migrants' lives, for as a child he heard stories of their travel and travail and learned of their dreams and hardships in Harlem, where he lived. He identified with Harlem so strongly that he experienced none of the alienation from the Black community felt by William H. Johnson and some other Black artists of the 1920s and 1930s. Indeed, when asked whether he considered what the Black community thought of his paintings, Lawrence answered without irony, "I am the Black community." Here was a man who eluded the social, aesthetic, and historical categories we commonly impose on art and artists, a man who had produced an open text that still speaks to us today.

Lawrence and his series were inspired more by literary mentors than by other visual artists. He trekked almost daily to the 135th Street Branch of the New York Public Library in 1940, consulted the work of writers, historians, and sociologists, and created the sixty panels of his *Migration* series from the inspiration of their words. The series was more than simply a work of art; it was part of a discourse on the meaning of the migration and on the African American experience that it epitomized from the second decade of the twentieth century until today. What Lawrence did was create a text that incorporated history, sociology, and a kind of poetry in a visual narrative that broke out of the typical categories of modern art.

A closer look at the relationship between Lawrence's work and his intellectual community reveals what eludes easy

Aaron Siskind. *Amateur Night, Apollo Theater, Harlem*. From the Photo League Feature Group project *Harlem Document*, which was exhibited in Harlem in 1939 (National Museum of American Art, Smithsonian Institution, gift of Tennyson and Fern Schad, courtesy Light Gallery)

Photographer unknown. 125th Street at 8th Avenue, Harlem, showing Apollo Theater, 1930s (New York Public Library, Local History Division)

categorization and empowers his visual message. A crucial part of his community was the corps of African American writers and intellectuals who had written extensively about the Black migration and the emerging role of the visual artist as an interpretive force in African American life and culture. In a sense, Lawrence incorporated all that had been thought and written about the migration in a series that went beyond those earlier texts.

Key among these individuals was Alain Le Roy Locke, a literary and visual arts critic, who wrote a letter of recommendation in 1940 for Lawrence's Rosenwald Fund fellowship to create the *Migration* series. Locke's letter is especially important because it helps to define the character of Lawrence's work. Locke described Lawrence as unique in his

ability to combine social interest and interpretation (he selects his own episodes from careful library reading and research) with a straight art approach when he comes to

work on his drawings. There is little or no hint of social propaganda in his pictures, and no slighting of the artistic problems involved, such as one finds in many of the contemporary social-theme painters. Yet his work has a stirring social and racial appeal.[2]

While some other critics, such as Charles Rogers, worried about the "strong tendency to propaganda" of Lawrence's project,[3] Locke argued that Lawrence's blending of art and "social interest" transformed social and political history into modern art. Later, Locke would note that a "warmly human but piercing social irony" was a "particularly characteristic" aspect of the series.[4]

The series not only advanced Lawrence's evolution as an artist; it also advanced our knowledge of the migration as a historical and a contemporary phenomenon. If, as art historian Richard Powell observed, "Lawrence's objective was an elucidation of social intercourse in history," he clarified our understanding of the Great Migration by painting it.[5] He moved, in my opinion, from artist to cultural interpreter of the first order. This function was precisely what Locke, early in his career, had defined as the special calling of the African American artist. It was one of the main reasons he was so enthusiastic about Lawrence. For Locke believed that African American art could be a redemptive force that could provide the Black community with the spiritual empowerment to fulfill its possibilities as a group and as a submerged nation in America. In *The New Negro* (1925), an anthology of Black writing that was deliberately subtitled "An Interpretation," Locke had argued that the artist was more important than the sociologist or the political leader to the self-understanding of the Black community, precisely because of this redemptive power. Toward that end, he urged artists during the Harlem Renaissance to transform the raw material of Black history and sociology into art. By the time Locke met Lawrence in the 1930s, the young artist was already doing—without a great deal of

Aaron Siskind. *Untitled*. From the project *The Most Crowded Block*, 1939–40 (National Museum of American Art, Smithsonian Institution, gift of Tennyson and Fern Schad, courtesy Light Gallery)

direction—what Locke had urged all along: creating art as a central means by which African Americans could achieve a profound understanding of themselves.

Born in Philadelphia in 1885, Locke belonged to a sophisticated urban African American middle class that had close ties with the educated elite of that Quaker city. His parents were part of an intellectual elite that instilled in its descendants a sense of duty to provide leadership for the Black community. As a child reared primarily by his mother, Locke imbibed her aesthetic sense, as reflected in the beautiful reproductions of famous artworks displayed in their home as well as her decorative sense of dress. Locke himself developed a particular fondness for pictures as a child, and by the time he graduated from Central High, Philadelphia's prestigious public high school, Locke was an aesthete, a lover of art of all kinds, who found greater satisfaction in aesthetic appreciation than in racial politics. After entering Harvard College in 1904 and graduating magna cum laude in philosophy in 1907, he became the first African American to be chosen as a Rhodes Scholar. At Oxford, rather than immerse himself in formal scholarship, Locke devoted himself to "personal culture," as he put it later, "but fortunately without enough money to collect blue china."[6] Like Bernard Berenson, another Harvard aesthete, he spent his time abroad studying paintings in the National Gallery of London, the Louvre, and dozens of small galleries and ateliers. He loved the work of such nineteenth-century English painters as Sir Joshua Reynolds, Thomas Gainsborough, and J.M.W. Turner, but he disliked the imitative traditionalism displayed by Henry O. Tanner, the Black expatriate artist, when he became essentially a religious painter in the early twentieth century.

Living abroad at the time of the birth of cubism, Locke frequented the Trocadero Museum and the less glamorous Parisian art galleries where African art was being exhibited and appreciated aesthetically for the first time. He had arrived in Europe without a firm concept of what a modern Afro-American visual art should be, but his sojourn convinced him that whatever Black art should become, it should be modern, informed by the African images and objects that had inspired Picasso and other modernists. He did not want Black American artists to imitate African art but to be inspired by it to turn away from academic classicism and create a contemporary Negro art grounded in their own

The "306 Group," in front of 306 West 141st Street, Charles Alston's Studio and gathering place for WPA artists, late 1930s. Standing, left to right: Addison Bates, Grace Richardson, Edgar Evans, Vertis Hayes, Alston, Cecil Gaylord, John Glenn, Elba Lightfoot, Selma Day, Ronald Joseph, Georgette Seabrook (Powell), Richard Reed. At front, left to right: Gwendolyn Knight (Lawrence), James Yeargens, Francisco Lord, Richard Lindsey, Frederick Coleman

experience and tradition. John Ruskin, writing about nineteenth-century British artists, expressed the ideals that Locke envisioned for twentieth-century African American artists. Modern British art, Ruskin concluded,

> must be got out of our own little island, and out of this year 1846, railroads and all: if a British painter, I say this in earnest seriousness, cannot make historical characters out of the British House of Peers, he cannot paint history; and if he cannot make a Madonna of a British girl of the nineteenth century, he cannot paint one at all."[7]

Locke hoped for a Black artist who could endow a portrait of an African American boy with the authenticity of a Baoule mask. But when he returned to the United States and began teaching at Howard University in 1912, the time was not right for a renaissance of Black visual art. There were too few African American artists, and, more important, most still worked within the classical tradition. Locke's conservative

Augusta Savage, teacher at the Harlem Art Workshop, 1930s (National Archives, Harmon Foundation Collection)

Charles Alston, early teacher and mentor of Lawrence, 1930s (National Archives, Harmon Foundation Collection)

aesthetic taste helped him appreciate the work of Meta Warrick Fuller, May Howard Jackson, and William Harper, but his knowledge of European modernism told him such work was too academic to become the basis of a modern Negro art in an age of cubism and abstraction. Moreover, their work did not directly engage the twentieth-century Black experience. But with the outbreak of World War I, the climate of opinion among the Black intelligentsia began to change, because thousands of southern Blacks migrated to the North, swelled the ghettos, and transformed the mood of the Black community. As Locke argued in "Harlem: Mecca of the New Negro," the special issue of the *Survey Graphic* that he edited (March 1, 1925), the physical migration symbolized a profound change in the "psychology of the masses." A new generation of "Afro-Americans" had shed the "Old Negro" attitude of gracious compliance with bigotry and now exhibited the proud and independent demeanor of the "New Negro." That new mood of racial pride infected

the young generation of writers Locke introduced in the *Survey Graphic* and in *The New Negro*, writers whose work he heralded as the beginning of a renaissance in Black letters.[8]

Sixteen years would pass, however, before a visual artist would emerge to portray the migration that Locke had argued was so crucial to twentieth-century African American racial consciousness. Despite the interval, Lawrence's *Migration* series echoed many of the themes that Locke had highlighted. Locke's interpretation, while informed by sociologists and historians, had rested on the notion that such a massive human movement should not be reduced to a sociological or economic phenomenon:

Neither labor demand, the boll-weevil nor the Ku Klux Klan is a basic factor, however contributary any or all of them may have been. The wash and rush of this human tide on the beach line of the northern city centers is to be explained primarily in terms of a new vision of a spirit to seize, even in the face of an extortionate and heavy toll, a chance for the improvement of conditions. With each successive wave of it, the movement of the Negro migrant becomes more and more like that of the European waves at their crests, a mass movement toward the larger and more democratic chance—in the Negro's case a deliberate flight not only from countryside to city, but from medieval America to modern.[9]

For Locke, the migration exemplified the agency of Black people, who had not fled conditions but seized opportunity and picked up their lives and belongings and moved en masse to freedom.

Although Lawrence's *Migration* series documented the economic pulls and pushes (panels 2, 4, 29, 31, 37, 44) and the social and political conditions of the migration (panels 15, 16, 17, 22, 49, 50), the largest number of panels portrayed this sense of agency. Some show Black people moving and taking charge of their lives instead of shrinking before social terrorism and inferior living conditions (panels 1, 3, 12, 18, 21, 23, 32, 35, 40, 60). While the series shows that Lawrence was quite familiar with historical and sociological studies of the migration—such as Emmett J. Scott's *Negro Migration During the War*, R. H. Heavell's Department of Labor–sponsored study, *Negro Migration in 1916–17*, and Carter G. Woodson's *A Century of Negro*

Aaron Douglas, noted modernist of the Harlem Renaissance, 1930s (National Archives, Harmon Foundation Collection)

Migration (1918)—it evokes more powerfully the way the Renaissance writers interpreted the movement.[10] Panel 56, a doctor examining a patient, reexpresses visually and verbally Locke's observation in "Harlem," the lead essay in the 1925 *Survey Graphic*, that it was "'the man's farthest down' who is most active in getting up. One of the most characteristic symptoms of this is the professional man himself migrating to recapture his constituency after a vain effort to maintain in some southern corner what for years seemed an established living and clientele."[11] Panels 3 and 40, in which people pass with their belongings in hand, present again what the novelist James Weldon Johnson in the same issue recalled he had seen with his own eyes in the South:

> I was in Jacksonville, Fla., for a while . . . and I sat one day and watched the stream of migrants passing to take the train. For hours they passed steadily, carrying flimsy suit cases, new and shiny, rusty old ones, bursting at the seams, boxes and bundles and impediments of all sorts, including banjos, guitars, birds in cages and what not.[12]

Indeed, Lawrence's panels also echoed themes explored by another Harlem Renaissance writer, Rudolph Fisher, whose series of vignettes on the migration, "The South Lingers On," also appeared in the "Harlem" issue. Fisher related the travail of an old sanctified preacher who travels to a northern city and rediscovers his parishioners, who entreat him to start up his church again. The story showed the importance of the church in the migrants' lives and illustrated Locke's point that traditional southern leaders were following their flock northward; Lawrence echoed these ideas in panels 54 and 56. But Lawrence also explored one of Fisher's more subtle themes—that despite (or because of?) their migration northward, the migrants remained connected emotionally and culturally to the South. The parishioners rush up to the "Rev'n Taylor" and begin to make plans to start a new church with him as the minister: "Martin an' Jim Lee's over to Ebeneezer, but dey doan like it 'tall. Says hit's too hifalutin for 'em, dass whut. Jes' come in an' set down an' git up and go out. Never moans, never shouts, never even says 'amen.'"[13] Fisher tells us that the migrants have retained their southern folkways, and Lawrence shows us this in several of his panels. In panel 45, for example, a migrant family sees Pittsburgh for the first time. The colors of their clothes, especially their hats, and the color and pattern of the

Jacob Lawrence. *Interior Scene*, 1937, tempera on paper
(collection of Philip J. and Suzanne Schiller)

Jacob Lawrence. "As a child, Toussaint heard the twang of the
planter's whip and saw blood stream from the bodies of slaves,"
panel 7, *Toussaint L'Ouverture* series, 1937–38, tempera on paper
(The Amistad Research Center, Aaron Douglas Collection, New
Orleans)

basket of food suggest southern designs and bright hues,
while the smiling faces and dramatic gestures convey the
excitement of fresh southern migrants as they enter northern
industrial civilization. Lawrence honors the migrants in a
symbolic sense by using bright colors and patterns to convey
the hopeful expectations they felt as they faced the urban
North. And he suggests as well that despite the urgent desire
to assimilate, these migrants will retain their southern culture
and fuse it with the northern culture they encounter.

Lawrence's view is linked to Fisher's by the sympathy both
express for the plight and trauma of the migrants. Generally,
sociologists and race leaders were not as kind, blaming the
migrants, in some cases, for the deterioration of northern
race relations and living conditions for northern Blacks.
Lawrence addresses the "old settlers'" attitude in panel 53,
where in the twisted mouths and bent faces of the well-
dressed man and woman we sense an attitude akin to E.
Franklin Frazier's condemnation of Harlem migrants as
"ignorant and unsophisticated peasant people without
experience [in] urban living."[14] The woman in the panel
could almost have been the woman historian Gilbert
Osofsky quoted: "Since the so-called 'Negro invasion,' the

property and character of everything have undergone a
change, and if you are honest, you will frankly acknowledge
it has not been for the improvement of the locality."[15]
Lawrence addressed that attitude, too, in the panels on
race riots (panels 49–51), but he avoided blaming the
Black masses.

The masses also brought new material and a new racial
consciousness to African American artists, who, like
Lawrence, began to conceive of their own role as creating
a grand narrative out of hundreds of individual stories. First,
there was the pioneering Aaron Douglas, who followed
Locke's injunction to create an African-inspired contemporary art in his illustrations for *The New Negro* and other
books and articles that appeared in the 1920s. By the early
1930s, Douglas was not alone: in "The American Negro as
Artist" (1931), Locke noted that many American Negro
artists had emerged whose art aimed "to express the race
spirit and background as well as the individual skill and
temperament of the artist."[16] He divided this new crop
of talent into the traditionalists, the modernists, and the
"Africanists, or Neo-Primitives, with the latter carrying the
burden of the campaign for a so-called 'Negro Art.'"[17]

Although the traditionalists remained popular, their predominance in the field was solidly challenged by such modernists as Archibald Motley, William H. Johnson, and Lillian Dorsey and by such "conscious 'Africanist[s]'" as James Lesesne Wells, Richmond Barthé, and Sargent Johnson. Although Locke cautioned, in a manner reminiscent of Ruskin, against "a sophisticated or forced exoticism" from Negro artists, he still welcomed and encouraged the notion that the formal qualities of art by the modernists and the Africanists laid the groundwork for a Black aesthetic. He argued that even in works that were not deliberately of a Negro subject, there often existed "subtler elements of rhythm, color and atmosphere" that distinguished the work of modern Negro artists.[18] The point was not that all African American art shared particular racial characteristics but rather that an aesthetic indigenous to the Black experience existed that could be legitimately developed by artists, whether African American or not. Locke believed the work of all Negro artists was strengthened by the presence of a significant subgroup who, like James Lesesne Wells, utilized "African motives and principles of design" in conceptualizing their work.[19]

Of the painters to emerge in the mid-1930s who elaborated the Black aesthetic, William H. Johnson was perhaps the most important for Locke. While not a protegé of Locke's, Johnson fused modernism and Africanism in a distinctive way that confirmed many of Locke's predictions. Locke promoted Johnson's art and career even more actively than he promoted Douglas's, for he served, through the Harmon Foundation and on his own, as Johnson's agent and broker. Ironically, their relationship ended when Johnson returned to the United States in 1938 and began to produce studies of the rural South that, in subject matter and formal qualities, most embodied what Locke wished to see in African American art. Several factors may have caused the rupture, not the least of which was Johnson's increasing criticism of Locke for his inability to sell the artist's work.

In the vacuum created by this disaffection, Lawrence emerged as the artist Locke believed most able to realize the promise of a self-consciously African American art. Like Johnson, Lawrence in his early works seemed fascinated with sharp design contrasts and the use of color to mold form. But he pushed the sculptural qualities of his compositions beyond the flat and spare use of space in Johnson's southern

series. In such early compositions as *Interior Scene* (1937), Lawrence created the illusion of three-dimensionality by infusing a flat, highly stylized design with sculptural qualities. He used sharp angles and bold color contrasts not only to suggest three-dimensionality but also to create a surreal stage on which the actors played out their scripted, seemingly hysterical roles. This composition looked back to the cardboard boxes that Lawrence had fashioned as a child after viewing acts at the Apollo Theater and looked forward to the angled interiors that would be the most powerful cubistic statements in the *Migration* series. Yet it was in his first series, on the life of the Haitian revolutionary Toussaint L'Ouverture (1937–38), that Lawrence pulled together all of his talents—his simplification and abstraction of forms, his manipulation of perspective, and his use of African design principles and ornamentation to create surface tensions—to create a text that came alive. When Locke wrote about the series in his 1939 article, "Advance on the Art Front," he emphasized its formal achievements as a work of art and its commitment to social values: "There is in truly great art no essential conflict between racial or national traits and universal human values."[20]

Locke offered that observation in part to rebut the growing number of younger artists who, in the late 1930s and early 1940s, rebelled against being called "Negro artists" and having their work considered as "Negro art," a classification they increasingly viewed as a stigmatizing ghetto. These artists also challenged Locke's notion of an African American aesthetic, to a certain extent because they wished their work to be considered solely as a part of American art. In *Modern Negro Art* (1941), the young Howard University art historian James A. Porter contested the notion that American Negro artists should be inspired by African art and that an African American aesthetic existed in the visual arts. Understandably, therefore, Lawrence's emergence in the early 1930s encouraged Locke, because Lawrence used African principles of design in his work and took as his subject African American history. Not since Aaron Douglas had Locke found an artist who was so comfortable with the educational value of his art.

Of course, like his contemporaries, Lawrence wanted to be taken seriously as an American artist. He resented those who referred to him patronizingly as the "best Negro artist," but he saw no conflict between the recognition that he was a

Jacob Lawrence (center) presenting a panel from his *Toussaint L'Ouverture* series to the registrar at the Baltimore Museum of Art, 1939 (National Archives, Harmon Foundation Collection)

great American artist and the idea that his work could be a transforming educational force in the Black community. It was uplifting to Locke to find such a talented artist who was not afraid to see himself—in the *Toussaint L'Ouverture* series and in the *Frederick Douglass* and *Harriet Tubman* series that followed—as a cultural interpreter of his people's history. While Locke's enthusiasm for Lawrence and his *Toussaint* series is evident from his published comments, his support for the *Migration* series is less well known because he published little on African American art in the 1940s and because most of his comments on Lawrence from that period have been buried in unpublished correspondence. Moreover, even his letter of recommendation to the Rosenwald Fund

avoided direct comment on the projected *Migration* series. He remarked only on the *Toussaint* series, which had created a "sensation" at the 1939 Baltimore Museum of Art show, noting that he and the museum director agreed the young artist possessed "a talent bordering on genius" and that Lawrence's more recent work showed "considerable growth in maturity and power over" the *Toussaint* series.[21]

Perhaps additional sources of Locke commentary on the *Migration* series will surface, but in their absence I want to suggest that his reticence may have derived from a degree of ambivalence. For while the series embodied much that Locke and others of his generation had to say about the migration, Lawrence brought to his narrative the feelings of a younger man who had grown up among migrants and who was an artist of the social realist tradition of the 1930s. Thus his interpretation critiqued the romanticism of earlier views of the migration and exposed the contradictions in the Promised Land. Ultimately, Lawrence's vision went beyond Locke's.

Lawrence's social criticism rescued him from the Harlem Renaissance generation's tendency to demean the migrants, on the one hand, for retaining too much of their "primitive" culture in the midst of modern urban life and to romanticize them, on the other, as a "folk" whose African-based culture would reform modern Western civilization. Without blaming the migrants, as E. Franklin Frazier did, or romanticizing the movement, as Locke tended to do, Lawrence highlighted the social conflict that accompanied the Great Migration. The scenes in panels 15, 17, 43, 50, and 52 address more directly than the art and literature of the 1920s Renaissance the issue of racial conflict; in them we feel the painful consequences of the decision to migrate and recall that many who tried to flee were blocked from leaving, beaten, arrested, and lynched for daring to leave the South. And it is not surprising that panels 45, 50, and 51, which depict the race riots, are among the most graphic of the series: Lawrence was living in Harlem when the 1935 riots erupted. On a thematic level, Lawrence is distinguished from other narrators of the migration for his ability to weave the personal and the political into these powerful visual metaphors.

Even Locke had to acknowledge in *The Negro in America* (1933) that both the migration and Harlem had begun to appear much less romantic. The health, housing, and working conditions of the migrants in the North had declined precipitously even before the onslaught of the Great Depression. In 1925, Locke had written that the migration represented the transition of African Americans from "medieval America to modern." Lawrence uses a variety of visual metaphors to show that the encounter with modernity came at a tremendous price. To evoke the barrenness of abandoned communities (panel 25) or the alienation of imprisonment (panel 41), the crush of overcrowding (panel 48), or the pain of terrorism (panels 15, 16), he uses a stark cubistic approach, a radical simplification of forms, to the point that even people become opaque and anonymous. Indeed, in some panels—such as panel 55, which depicts

pallbearers carrying a coffin—Lawrence's reduction of the image of the migrants to the sparsest of forms captures metaphorically the way in which social forces reduced the migrants' life chances.

Yet Lawrence refuses to leave us in despair. In panel 47, which shows nine children squeezed in one bed in a tenement apartment, he achieves a synthetic, redemptive image of a people at the crossroads. While the cubic blank walls suggest the barrenness of northern urban life, the bed's beautiful quilt with its bright colors and patterns recalls the southern folk tradition. Lawrence suggests that we need to hold on to that past, just as he has held on to the color, design, and pattern of southern decorative culture in his modernist palette. For only through a sense of cultural continuity and narrative connection with their past, Lawrence tells us, can a people remain psychically grounded in modern life.

Why is Lawrence's rendering the best narrative that we have of the migration? Why do I find his interpretation more compelling than Alain Locke's or E. Franklin Frazier's or even Rudolph Fisher's? Of course, Lawrence is a supremely talented artist. Yet even within Lawrence's oeuvre, the *Migration* series stands out as his finest work. The answer, I believe, lies in his own life.

As a child of migrants, Lawrence could recapture a sense of the events he had heard about as a child. Lawrence's intimacy with his subject matter is reflected in the most striking formal characteristic of the series: the way it portrays the migration as something we witness ourselves, as if it is happening right before us. While this sort of rendering is not exclusive to the *Migration* series—some early attempts at such a perspective occur in the *Toussaint* series—Lawrence used it more frequently and more effectively here, perhaps because of his emotional connection to the events. We are there on the platform, as in panel 39, watching the crowd of migrants approach the station. We are in line, in panel 59, waiting to vote under the watchful eye of a cop. And we are watching, in panel 33, as a woman lies on a bed reading a letter from a migrant. This conceit is present even when people are not, as in panel 48, where the crowded beds in a Harlem apartment can be imagined as seen from the perspective of a little child searching for his or her bed. Remarkably, Lawrence the adult artist recaptured the wonder of a child who had seen the migrants, watched his parents, and observed the Harlem environment from inside. And through his eye and his art, we identify emotionally with a community that Lawrence saw as his own.

NOTES

1. On June 3, 1992, The Phillips Collection hosted a meeting and discussion with Jacob Lawrence for Henry Louis Gates, Jr., Patricia Hills, Richard Powell, Diane Tepfer, Deborah Willis, me, and several other museum professionals and consultants.

   "Black" is capitalized here because it refers to an ethnic minority. White is not capitalized because it does not refer to such an ethnic minority.

2. Alain Locke to Julius Rosenwald Fund, "Confidential Report on Candidate for Fellowship," re Jacob Armstead Lawrence, January 23, 1940, Rosenwald Fund Collection, Special Collections, Fisk University, Nashville, Tenn. (hereafter Rosenwald Fund Collection). I am indebted to Diane Tepfer for bringing this material to my attention.

3. Charles Rogers (director, Baltimore Museum of Art) to Julius Rosenwald Fund, "Confidential Report on Candidate for Fellowship," re Jacob Armstead Lawrence, n. d., Rosenwald Fund Collection.

4. Alain Locke, "Up Till Now," in *The Negro Artist Comes of Age: A National Survey of Contemporary American Artists* (exhibition catalogue, Albany Institute of History and Art, January 3–February 11, 1945), reprinted in Jeffrey C. Stewart, ed., *The Critical Temper of Alain Locke: A Selection of His Essays on Art and Culture* (New York: Garland Publishing, 1982), 193–94.

5. Richard J. Powell, *Jacob Lawrence* (New York: Rizzoli, 1992), [1].

6. "Alain Le Roy Locke," *Harvard Class of 1908, 2nd Class Report* (Cambridge: Harvard College, 1914), 207. He chose to remain a member of the class of 1908 even though he left with his degree in 1907.

7. John Ruskin, *Of General Principles and of Truth*, vol. 1 of *Modern Painters* (1873; New York: E. P. Dutton, 1935), 115–16.

8. Alain Locke, "Harlem," *Survey Graphic* 51 (March 1, 1925): 629–30.

9. Ibid.

10. Scott, *Negro Migration During the War* (New York: Oxford University Press, 1920); Heavell et al., *Negro Migration in 1916–17* (1919; New York: Negro Universities Press, 1969); Woodson, *A Century of Negro Migration* (1918; New York: AMS Press, 1970), 167–211.

11. Locke, "Harlem," 630.

12. James Weldon Johnson, "The Making of Harlem," *Survey Graphic* 51 (March 1, 1925): 636.

13. Rudolph Fisher, "The South Lingers On," *Survey Graphic* 51 (March 1, 1925): 645.

14. Quoted in Gilbert Osofsky, *Harlem: The Making of a Ghetto* (New York: Harper and Row, 1966), 139.

15. Ibid., 140.

16. Alain Locke, "The American Negro as Artist," *American Magazine of Art* 23 (September 1931): 213–14, reprinted in Stewart, *Critical Temper*, 173–74.

17. Locke, "Advance on the Art Front," *Opportunity* 17 (May 1939): 133, reprinted in Stewart, *Critical Temper*, 176.

18. Alain Locke, foreword to *Contemporary Negro Art* (exhibition catalogue, Baltimore Museum of Art, February 3–19, 1939), [3], reprinted in Stewart, *Critical Temper*, 183.

19. Locke, "Advance," 177

20. Ibid.

21. Locke to Rosenwald Fund.

The Migration Series

1. During the World War there was a great migration North by Southern Negroes.

2. The World War had caused a great shortage in Northern industry and also citizens of foreign countries were returning home.

3. In every town Negroes were leaving by the hundreds to go North and enter into Northern industry.

4. The Negro was the largest source of labor to be found after all others had been exhausted.

5. The Negroes were given free passage on the railroads which was paid back by Northern industry. It was an agreement that the people brought North on these railroads were to pay back their passage after they had received jobs.

6. The trains were packed continually with migrants.

7. The Negro, who had been part of the soil for many years, was now going into and living a new life in the urban centers.

8. They did not always leave because they were promised work in the North. Many of them left because of Southern conditions, one of them being great floods that ruined the crops, and therefore they were unable to make a living where they were.

9. Another great ravager of the crops was the boll weevil.

10. They were very poor.

11. In many places, because of the war, food had doubled in price.

12. The railroad stations were at times so over-packed with people leaving that special guards had to be called in to keep order.

12

13. Due to the South's losing so much of its labor, the crops were left to dry and spoil.

13

14. Among the social conditions that existed which was partly the cause of the migration was the injustice done to the Negroes in the courts.

15. Another cause was lynching. It was found that where there had been a lynching, the people who were reluctant to leave at first left immediately after this.

16. Although the Negro was used to lynching, he found this an opportune time for him to leave where one had occurred.

17. The migration was spurred on by the treatment of the tenant farmers by the planter.

18. The migration gained in momentum.

19. There had always been discrimination.

20. In many of the communities the Negro press was read continually because of its attitude and its encouragement of the movement.

21. Families arrived at the station very early in order not to miss their train North.

22. Another of the social causes of the migrants' leaving was that at times they did not feel safe, or it was not the best thing to be found on the streets late at night. They were arrested on the slightest provocation.

23. And the migration spread.

23

24. Child labor and a lack of education was one of the other reasons for people wishing to leave their homes.

25. After a while some communities were left almost bare.

26. And people all over the South began to discuss this great movement.

27. Many men stayed behind until they could bring their families North.

28. The labor agent who had been sent South by Northern industry was a very familiar person in the Negro counties.

29. The labor agent also recruited laborers to break strikes which were occurring in the North.

30. In every home people who had not gone North met and tried to decide if they should go North or not.

31. After arriving North the Negroes had better housing conditions.

32. The railroad stations in the South were crowded with people leaving for the North.

33. People who had not yet come North received letters from their relatives telling them of the better conditions that existed in the North.

34. The Negro press was also influential in urging the people to leave the South.

35. They left the South in large numbers and they arrived in the North in large numbers.

36. They arrived in great numbers into Chicago, the gateway of the West.

37. The Negroes that had been brought North worked in large numbers in one of the principal industries, which was steel.

38. They also worked in large numbers on the railroad.

39. Luggage crowded the railroad platforms.

40. The migrants arrived in great numbers.

41 . The South that was interested in keeping cheap labor was making it very difficult for labor agents recruiting Southern labor for Northern firms. In many instances, they were put in jail and were forced to operate incognito.

42. They also made it very difficult for migrants leaving the South. They often went to railroad stations and arrested the Negroes wholesale, which in turn made them miss their trains.

43. In a few sections of the South the leaders of both groups met and attempted to make conditions better for the Negro so that he would remain in the South.

46. Industries attempted to board their labor in quarters that were oftentimes very unhealthy. Labor camps were numerous.

46

47. As well as finding better housing conditions in the North, the migrants found very poor housing conditions in the North. They were forced into overcrowded and dilapidated tenement houses.

48. Housing for the Negroes was a very difficult problem.

49. They also found discrimination in the North although it was much different from that which they had known in the South.

50

50. Race riots were very numerous all over the North because of the antagonism that was caused between the Negro and white workers. Many of these riots occurred because the Negro was used as a strike breaker in many of the Northern industries.

51. In many cities in the North where the Negroes had been overcrowded in their own living quarters they attempted to spread out. This resulted in many of the race riots and the bombing of Negro homes.

52. One of the largest race riots occurred in East St. Louis.

52

53. The Negroes who had been North for quite some time met their fellowmen with disgust and aloofness.

53

54. One of the main forms of social and recreational activities in which the migrants indulged occurred in the church.

55. The Negro being suddenly moved out of doors and cramped into urban life, contracted a great deal of tuberculosis. Because of this the death rate was very high.

56. Among one of the last groups to leave the South was the Negro professional who was forced to follow his clientele to make a living.

57. The female worker was also one of the last groups to leave the South.

58. In the North the Negro had better educational facilities.

59. In the North the Negro had freedom to vote.

60. And the migrants kept coming.

60

Edith Halpert in her living room, ca. 1940s (Downtown Gallery Papers, Archives of American Art, Smithsonian Institution)

Edith Gregor Halpert:
Impresario of Jacob Lawrence's *Migration* Series

DIANE TEPFER

When Alain Locke, Howard University professor of philosophy and theoretician of the Harlem Renaissance, showed Jacob Lawrence's *Migration* series to Edith Gregor Halpert, founder of New York's pioneering commercial Downtown Gallery, Halpert was so dazzled that she arranged for *Fortune* magazine to publish part of the series as a portfolio, made plans to show the entire series at her gallery, and prepared to enlist special patrons to carry out her mission of properly "placing" the series. As impressive as this reception and later "placement" in The Phillips Memorial Gallery and The Museum of Modern Art was some fifty years ago, the activity was entirely in character for Edith Halpert, an extraordinary dealer of American art.

Lawrence and his aesthetics appealed intensely to Halpert because, like Lawrence, she was an American original, and as a woman, a Jew, and an immigrant, she too had contended with outsider status. Halpert's formative years reveal similarities with Lawrence's. Both came to Harlem as children with their mothers and a sibling, both were precocious and hardworking, and both became extremely successful. In 1906 Edith Gregor Fiviosioovitch (1900–70) came to America from Odessa, Russia, and settled in Harlem, then a center of middle-class immigrant Jewish life. Her widowed mother opened a candy store, where Edith first learned merchandising. An aspiring artist, Edith enrolled at the age of fourteen in the National Academy of Design; by seventeen she was supporting herself by working in advertising at department stores. In 1918 she married the early American modernist artist Samuel Halpert. In 1926 she combined her department store marketing skills with the entrée into the art world she had acquired from Sam and his friends: instead of making art herself, she opened an art gallery.[1]

Halpert was in pursuit of a new definition of American art and a new constituency. Her Downtown Gallery was located in Greenwich Village, where many artists worked, away from the intimidating atmosphere of traditional uptown galleries. Its nontraditional mission was to make American art available to all at low prices. Before the Downtown Gallery opened, most dealers specialized in European art or, at the very least, in artists who had worked in Europe. In 1926 there was no Whitney Museum of American Art, no Museum of Modern Art, and the Phillips Memorial Gallery had just begun to show modern art and its sources. By the end of her first season, Halpert had learned two things: a market for contemporary American art existed all over the United States, and the best way to make that art accessible was to place it in the museums that were opening or expanding everywhere.

From the outset Halpert astutely made connections with a variety of influential people and devised ways to involve them in her efforts. Her most significant and successful strategy was to use nineteenth-century folk art, such as Edward Hicks's *Peaceable Kingdom*, and indigenous forms, including weather vanes, to help finance the work of living artists and to serve as what Halpert termed "American ancestors." With Holger Cahill, later director of the Federal Art Project, she formulated a program to collect, publicize, and market folk art in the Downtown Gallery's American Folk Art Gallery. The gallery's most consequential client was Abby Aldrich Rockefeller (Mrs. John D. Rockefeller, Jr.), who would found The Museum of Modern Art with two women friends within a year and a half after meeting Halpert. From Rockefeller's substantial collection, purchased from Halpert, Cahill organized exhibitions of "Primitives" (1930) and "American Folk Art" (1931) at the Newark Museum and "Art of the Common Man" (1932) at The Museum of Modern Art.

Rockefeller also gave commissions to Downtown Gallery artists, including Charles Sheeler, Marguerite Zorach, and Ben Shahn, and financial help, often anonymously with Halpert's intercession, to Hale Woodruff, Arshile Gorky, and others. One of the most ambitious of Halpert's many strategies to promote the welfare of living artists was the vast First New York Municipal Art Exhibition in 1934, for which she negotiated space in Rockefeller Center from Nelson Rockefeller in exchange for the endorsement of Mayor Fiorello La Guardia, which Halpert duly secured.

Holger Cahill brought Halpert to Washington during the summer of 1936 to package traveling exhibitions assembled from the various state art projects. The Exhibition and Allotment Program Halpert directed was located in Studio House, the school of the Phillips Memorial Gallery; Duncan Phillips, a regular visitor to the Downtown Gallery and sometimes a client, was a great supporter of the Federal Art Project. From among thousands of works by young artists, Halpert helped plan the landmark exhibition "New Horizons in American Art," shown at The Museum of Modern Art. For the Downtown Gallery she selected a crop of promising artists from outside New York. The work ranged from the social commentary of Jack Levine's figure paintings to the eerie unpopulated precisionist landscapes of Edmund Lewandowski.

In the midst of the depression, the Downtown Gallery mounted several financially successful shows. Halpert's taste and inclinations stretched from the social statements of Ben Shahn's *Sacco and Vanzetti* series to the rediscovery of the stunning late-nineteenth-century trompe l'oeil still-life painter William Harnett. At the beginning of the 1940–41 season Halpert moved the gallery uptown to a handsome townhouse at 43 East 51st Street, which she converted into a stylish and up-to-date setting for art. The gallery retained its progressive values, but the move signified Halpert's desire for Establishment acclaim for the Downtown Gallery and the art and artists she showed there.

In 1941 Halpert read *The Negro in Art*, the recently published volume by Alain Le Roy Locke, which was illustrated with a large selection of nineteenth- and twentieth-century art.[2] She became especially ardent about the nineteenth-century artists she encountered for the first time, perceiving them as "background material" for the contemporary Negro artists she already knew through her

"W.P.A. contacts." Halpert enthusiastically wrote Locke in June 1941 that she wanted to "introduce Negro art in a large inclusive exhibition" with his consultation.[3] Her approach would be similar to her successful promotion of nineteenth-century white artists as the "American ancestors" of the contemporary artists she handled. The exhibition would involve an educational component to "demonstrate to the public the valuable contribution made by American Negro artists,"[4] displaying one painting by each of five little-known artists—Edward M. Bannister (1828–1901), Robert S. Duncanson (1821–71), Edwin A. Harleston (1882–1931), William H. Simpson (1818–72), and Henry O. Tanner (1859–1937)—together with works by contemporary "Negro" artists.

Halpert's collaboration with Locke had begun more than ten years earlier. Between 1929 and 1931 the Downtown Gallery joined other cultural mavericks and philanthropists in supporting an artistic residency in France for Hale Woodruff, whom Locke had introduced to Halpert in 1927.[5] As the visionary of the "New Negro Movement," Locke declared the power of art based on the rediscovery of cultural roots in Africa rather than on images of the "happy slave" or on styles merely assimilated from Western culture.

Locke responded eagerly to Halpert's proposal, and he worked with her for six months on this monumental project.[6] Their collaboration would have a notable consequence: the art of Jacob Lawrence would eagerly be taken into the canon of significant contemporary Americana.

Shortly after Locke's response he brought her photographs of the work of Jacob Lawrence. It is surprising that Halpert was not yet aware of Lawrence's work, for the twenty-three-year-old artist had already received professional recognition. He had participated in three one-artist exhibitions and more than ten group exhibitions, and his work, although firmly based on his experience of his own heritage and community, had already reached a specialized cross-over audience. He had been a scholarship student at the progressive American Artists School between 1936 and 1938. His forty-one-panel *Toussaint L'Ouverture* series (1937–38) had been given an entire room in the Baltimore Museum of Art's 1939 exhibition "Contemporary Negro Art" and was next shown in New York in a solo exhibition at the De Porres Interracial Center. The following year, Lawrence was awarded second prize in the art exhibition accompanying the Chicago

American Negro Exposition. In New York, he had a one-artist exhibition at Columbia University's East Hall, where the *Toussaint* series was again shown.[7]

Closer to Halpert's milieu, admirers of Lawrence were to be found at The Museum of Modern Art. Jay Leyda, assistant curator of the Film Department, liked the narrative format of Lawrence's historical series and encouraged him in his work. He introduced Lawrence to passionate expressionist film, such as von Stroheim's *Blue Angel*, and to other art professionals, including Lincoln Kirstein, director of Ballet Caravan; Holger Cahill; José Clemente Orozco, the Mexican muralist; Dorothy Miller, assistant curator of painting and sculpture at The Museum of Modern Art; and possibly Alfred Barr, founding director of the museum. Leyda also supported Lawrence's successful application for his first Rosenwald fellowship in 1940 and solicited recommendations for it from his colleagues.[8]

Jacob Lawrence's fellowship, which was renewed in 1941 and 1942, supported his research at the Schomburg Collection and the painting of the *Migration* series. The fund created by Julius Rosenwald, an extraordinary and innovative philanthropist, gave more than four hundred fellowships to African Americans between 1928 and 1948; the largest group of fellows were in the fine arts. Whether consciously or unconsciously, in her support of African American artists Halpert sought to join this larger network created by Rosenwald and other prominent members of the Jewish community.[9]

Recognizing the timeliness of Lawrence's series, Halpert quickly brought it to the attention of Deborah Calkins, *Fortune* magazine's visionary and efficient assistant art director. Halpert knew that *Fortune* had the interest and resources to package and present the series to a prestigious and influential audience. The previous December the magazine had published *Power*, an impressive portfolio of six portraits of energy-generating machines commissioned from Charles Sheeler, a senior Downtown Gallery artist.[10] Halpert, Locke, and Calkins probably viewed the *Migration* panels together at the Harlem Community Art Center on June 25, 1941. Soon thereafter, Calkins and the editors of *Fortune* advised Lawrence that they would publish the series "in the fall or winter—unless the war situation makes publication obsolete."[11] Halpert adamantly negotiated with the magazine to ensure that Lawrence received a $150 option

and eventually a total of $500; *Fortune* also contributed $100 to the Negro Art Fund, which Halpert planned to create at the Downtown Gallery.

Calkins reported to Locke in late August 1941 that Lawrence's work was scheduled for the November issue and requested reading material for the magazine's customary "well-documented background." Locke lent her a copy of his book, *The Negro in America*, directing her to the section on "the present-day problem," which he felt concisely presented his view "on the significance of migration, and its possibilities as a new front of race contacts with American life."[12] These ideas are echoed in the text written collectively by staff to accompany the twenty-six panels reproduced in the November 1941 issue. The elegant, full-color portfolio was entitled "'. . . And the Migrants Kept Coming': A Negro artist paints the story of the great American minority."

Lawrence and Halpert did not actually meet until he returned from his first stay in the South. But from August 1941 to May 1942, while he lived in New Orleans and in Lenexa, Virginia, with his new wife, the painter Gwendolyn Clarine Knight, he and Halpert corresponded regularly. Their surviving letters and those between Lawrence and Locke have given scholars a rich written record that probably would not be available had Lawrence remained in New York. From their first dealings Halpert solicited and respected Lawrence's decisions about the price and disposition of his work. She did not follow her usual practice and lower Lawrence's prices to induce sales. When she asked how he felt about selling the panels of the *Migration* series singly or together, he replied:

> I have finally decided not to break up the series. I have reached this conclusion because the complete story was conceived within the sixty paintings, therefore to sell any one painting would make it an incomplete story. I also know the difficulty of selling the entire set as a whole. I have fixed a price of $2,000 for the complete set.[13]

However, when Lawrence saw the *Fortune* piece, he realized that a careful selection could make a meaningful ensemble. He wrote Halpert, "I was very pleased with the job they did on the whole lay out. I thought that the story of the migration was complete and that the accompanying article and notes were very good."[14]

Halpert's elaborate preparations for the December 1941

Twenty-six panels from Jacob Lawrence's *Migration* series as they appeared in the November 1941 issue of *Fortune* magazine

"In spite of everything, living conditions were better in the North. The Negro professional followed his clientele up from the South."

"Gradually female workers also began to come to the North."

"In the church the migrants found one of their main sources of recreation and of social artistry."

"In the North the Negro had freedom to vote . . . In the North the Negro had better educational facilities."

THOUGH economically prostrate, the northern Negro at least can vote, send his children to school, and move about with some freedom. Consequently, he is much more of a man than his southern brother. But while he is hoved up in a semighetto, and while the white world conspires to prevent him from earning a living, he is in no sense a democratic man living in a democracy. He knows this, and so do others. In every country in the world Hitler has used the American Negro as prime propaganda to convince people that U.S. democracy is a mockery.

But even in the segregation and discrimination he endures the Negro is finding strength. If he cannot achieve dignity in the eyes of the whites, he can create a racial pride that somewhat compensates—and he does. If he cannot make any individual headway in a white world, he can make collective headway if he learns to make the weight of his numbers felt—and he is learning. He has the ballot—millions of ballots—and in recent years he has swung more than a few cities and perhaps a few states. He would be ready now to rally around a leader he could understand—a Negro Huey Long—and if he gets kicked around much longer he will probably find one.

. . . and the migrants kept coming."

"The Negroes, who had been part of the soil for many years, arrived in great numbers in the urban centers of the North."

"Cramped into urban life, they contracted a great deal of tuberculosis. The death rate was very high."

"The vast numbers of migrants made housing difficult. They were overcrowded in dilapidated tenement houses."

"Sometimes to keep migrants from leaving they were held in the railroad station and made to miss the train."

"There were race riots. They happened because the Negroes tried to move into new neighborhoods, or because of antagonism between the Negro and the white workers. Often the Negro was used as a strike-breaker in northern plants. The worst riot occurred in East St. Louis."

"The Negroes who were already in the North met their fellow men with disgust and aloofness."

"In many cities, when they attempted to spread out, Negro homes were bombed."

"American Negro Art" exhibition at the Downtown Gallery were jeopardized by what she feared would be a somewhat imitative, and possibly rival, exhibition at the Mc Millen Interior Decoration and Art Gallery. This exhibition, Halpert convinced Locke, threatened to steal their thunder and pervert their cause. Halpert had intended "to introduce a representative cross section of the work of Negro artists, both to the art critics in New York and to several important museum directors." But they learned from Peter Pollack, head of the South Side Art Center in Chicago, that the urbane Frank Crowninshield—editor of *Vanity Fair*, founding trustee of The Museum of Modern Art, and owner of a substantial collection of African sculpture assembled by the artist John Graham—was "broke and is trying to sell his African collection [within an] exhibition of contemporary

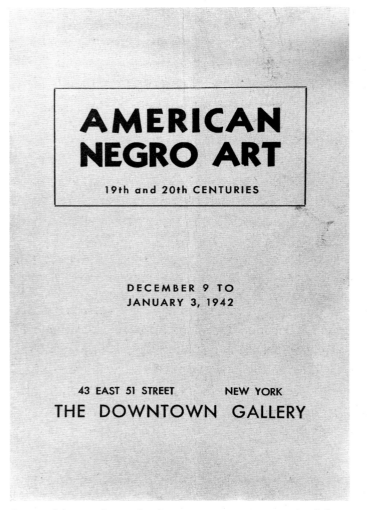

AMERICAN NEGRO ART

19th and 20th CENTURIES

DECEMBER 9 TO
JANUARY 3, 1942

43 EAST 51 STREET   NEW YORK

THE DOWNTOWN GALLERY

Cover of the catalogue for the "American Negro Art" exhibition at Edith Halpert's Downtown Gallery, December 1941 (National Archives, Harmon Foundation Collection)

Negro art . . . to publicize the African stuff." When Mc Millen curator Kathleen Carroll went to Chicago to select paintings, an unfortunate argument developed between artists who believed they would receive a better price by contributing to Mc Millen, the first exhibition, and those who would go with the Downtown Gallery's credentials.[15]

Despite the disdain of Halpert and her allies, Mc Millen mounted "Negro Art, Contemporary," October 16–November 7, 1941. An *Art Digest* article on the Mc Millen show noted "a sudden emphasis on the art of the U.S. Negro." Unlike the forthcoming Downtown Gallery exhibition, the show included "the pure African background of 'Negro' art."[16] Halpert also objected to the association Mc Millen and others made between contemporary Negro art and what she termed "Savage art." Following the teachings of Locke, she preferred instead a grouping with American folk art. Indeed, in a photograph of the Downtown Gallery installation, the bottom of a weather vane is visible above Robert Duncanson's *Blue Hole, Little Miami River* (oil, 1851). Despite Halpert's anxiety, the Mc Millen show has been overshadowed in the history of American art by the Downtown Gallery's exhibition.

Because the *Migration* series generated such extraordinary appeal and enthusiasm, Halpert modified her original plan and showed it first in November, at the time of its publication in *Fortune*. In a departure from her usual practice, she deliberately did not seek reviews but rather directed the press release to the forthcoming "American Negro Art" exhibition. She told Lawrence, "We have not made too great an issue of these as we want to save the excitement for the large show . . . . At that time we have some special plans in connection with the group. What with the Mc Millen show, we decided to hold off the real fire works until December."[17] Her plan was to have the Downtown Gallery and other New York galleries add one contemporary Negro artist to each of their rosters; she would also establish a Negro Art Fund to purchase art for public collections.

The special character of "American Negro Art" brought added cachet through a prestigious and glamorous sponsorship committee that Halpert and Locke assembled. The list in the brochure began with Mrs. Franklin Delano Roosevelt and the Honorable Fiorello H. La Guardia. Other luminaries included Katherine Dunham, pioneer of modern

The *Migration* series on view at the Downtown Gallery, 1941 (National Archives, Harmon Foundation Collection)

African American dance; Edsel Ford, president of Ford Motor Company, and Eleanor Clay Ford, art patron; Dr. David Levy, noted child psychologist, and Adele Rosenwald Levy; A. Philip Randolph, founding president of the Brotherhood of Sleeping Car Porters; William (Bill "Bojangles") Robinson, king of tap dancers; John D. Rockefeller, Jr., and Abby Aldrich Rockefeller; and Carl Van Vechten, author, portrait photographer, and music critic. Alain Locke headed the Coordination Committee roster, which included Lawrence Allen, the Downtown Gallery's longtime African American secretary.[18]

On the first page of the brochure, Halpert explained the Negro Art Fund:

> The Downtown Gallery has two objectives in presenting this exhibition. One is to continue its educational program by demonstrating to the public the valuable contribution made by American Negro artists. The second objective—a vital one—is to inaugurate a special NEGRO ART FUND for the purchase of paintings, sculpture, and graphics by contemporary American Negro artists, such works to be presented to museums and other public institutions. You can help by either making a direct donation, or by purchasing works of art on exhibition. The Gallery is contributing the entire sales commissions, as well as all its facilities.[19]

Several photographs commissioned and preserved by the Harmon Foundation document the gracious installation of the *Migration* panels. In one view, ten panels are mounted in two rows in Halpert's coffered wood-paneled office. They are flanked by Eldzier Corter's *Southern Landscape* (tempera, 1940) and by John H. Smith's *Self-Portrait* (cast stone, 1934) on the adjacent mantel. Curiously, the installation does not follow the sequence of the series; one row is all horizontal panels, the other all vertical, rather than the more rhythmic sequence the artist specified. Several other photographs show more panels in a spare, yet elegant, modernized room; another documents Romare Bearden's *After Church* (tempera, 1941), Sargent Johnson's *Chester*

Edith Halpert with a group of Downtown Gallery artists and their work, photographed for *Life* magazine, March 17, 1952. Behind Halpert are (from left): Charles Oscar, Robert Knipschild, Jonah Kinigsten, Wallace Reiss, Carroll Cloar, and Herbert Katzman (photo by Louis Faurer).

(terra cotta, 1929), and other twentieth-century painting and sculpture from the exhibition. Visible below are *Fortune* magazine open to the *Migration* series, Locke's *The Negro in Art*, discreet placards reading, "All exhibits are for sale," and other supplementary material.

The Harmon Foundation's photographs are rare documents because Halpert usually did not take installation photographs of exhibitions in her gallery. The foundation's pioneering art exhibitions and other activities helped encourage and support many African American artists. Mary Beattie Brady, the foundation's devoted director, was a dedicated supporter of Jacob Lawrence. In 1939 she purchased his *Toussaint L'Ouverture* series and made it available for loan exhibitions. The practical services she faithfully provided helped Lawrence and other artists focus on making art.[20]

The bombing of Pearl Harbor and the immediate entry of the United States into World War II eclipsed the carefully planned December 8 opening and the exhibition itself. But, although Halpert's educational aim was never fully realized, "American Negro Art" was important to Romare Bearden, Elizabeth Catlett, and the forty-five other contemporary painters, printmakers, and sculptors who had an opportunity to show their works at the Downtown Gallery.[21] Halpert also

included two works that Jacob Lawrence had created recently in the South: *The Green Table* and *Catholic New Orleans*. While most of the earlier works were loaned from public collections and not for sale, no other exhibition at that time had shown as many museum-quality works and included both nineteenth- and twentieth-century examples.

Halpert did not have to work hard to promote the *Migration* series; Lawrence's art seemed almost to sell itself. Rather, she devoted her skill and ingenuity to placing the series in two major collections. By the close of the exhibition, she had persuaded Adele Rosenwald Levy—the daughter of Julius Rosenwald and a philanthropist, community and social service leader, and member of The Museum of Modern Art Board of Trustees—to purchase thirty panels and donate them as her first gift to the museum. Halpert wrote Levy:

Apart from the documentary importance of this group, the aesthetic quality is such that a good many authorities in the art world consider the series one of the most important contributions to contemporary art. Jacob Lawrence was enabled to produce these paintings through the fellowship of the Rosenwald Foundation. Both the artist and I . . . feel that it would benefit not only the Museum and its public, but the artist and his race.[22]

Alfred Barr later wrote to Levy that he had selected the even-numbered panels because they include "the staircase picture you liked so much [no. 46]."[23]

Duncan Phillips bought the odd-numbered panels for The Phillips Memorial Gallery. Halpert knew of Phillips's early appreciation of Horace Pippin, a contemporary African American folk artist who would soon show at the Downtown Gallery. Both Phillips and Levy paid, according to Halpert, "a ridiculously low price . . . one thousand dollars, or at an average of $33. per panel," and Lawrence received his price of $2,000, less a 33 percent commission to the Negro Art Fund. Halpert provided the "captions" Lawrence wrote and suggested they be placed on the wooden framing strips. She expressed her hope that "the entire series will be preserved for the future and will be useful for educational work both in the field of art and in the field of racial history."[24] The Phillips and The Museum of Modern Art agreed that each institution would lend its half to the other to facilitate the exhibition of the entire series.

The *Migration* series first went on exhibition at the Phillips in March 1942 and then was circulated by MoMA to fourteen small museums around the United States between October 1942 and June 1944. The press release suggests the expanded meanings Lawrence's series would bear during World War II and the resulting influx of refugees throughout Europe and the Americas:

Today nearly half of all American Negroes (one-tenth of our population) are city dwellers.

Though they constitute a far larger minority group than any on the European continent, and though they represent a social and economic enigma of tremendous proportions, the 13 million Negroes in this country are citizens of a shadowy sub-nation that is unknown to, or overlooked by, most of the rest of our population.

The Museum of Modern Art showed the entire series in its Auditorium Gallery from October 10 through November 5, 1944, together with eight new paintings Lawrence had made during his Coast Guard service. The museum invested the series with the sinister overtones of events that had not yet occurred when it was created. A draft for the wall panel reads:

Life called this group of Downtown Gallery artists "oldtimers." Some had been with the gallery since its opening in 1926. Seated, from left, are Jack Levine (on floor), Stuart Davis (behind Levine), William Zorach, and Bernard Karfiol. Behind them are Jacob Lawrence, David Fredenthal, Yasuo Kuniyoshi, Charles Sheeler, and Ben Shahn (photo by Louis Faurer).

In every country in the world, Hitler has used the American Negro as prime propaganda to convince people that U.S. democracy is a mockery. To bring these facts to the attention of those within our own borders at the same time [as] they are being carried to the ends of the earth in our battle against the tyranny of a Nazi world was the aim of the department of circulating exhibitions in making this show available to institutions throughout the United States. . . . [W]e hope these eloquent statements by Jacob Lawrence have caused many Americans to examine their democratic beliefs.[25]

By helping to place the *Migration* series in these two important museums, Edith Halpert furthered her goal of broad exposure for American Negro art and prestige for the Downtown Gallery. Lawrence, who had created four major series before he came to Halpert's attention, would have continued to make his art whether or not the Downtown Gallery had discovered him. Some time earlier, when the government of Haiti expressed an interest in acquiring the *Toussaint* series, Lawrence had written to Locke:

137

I think it means much more to an artist to have people like and enjoy his work, than it does to have a few individuals purchase his work, and it not have the interest of the masses.[26]

Through the auspices of the Downtown Gallery and the two museums, Lawrence realized his hope for wide public access to his work. He always acknowledged the importance of his early association with the Downtown Gallery:

Edith Halpert was greatly responsible for me and my early success and I would think my latest success, because if it hadn't been for the early success. . . . And this is how it all started and how I became more a part of the art world.[27]

NOTES

I want to acknowledge the critical leadership of Elizabeth Hutton Turner in the development of this project. It has been a treat to collaborate with the extremely helpful team of scholars she assembled, Jacob and Gwendolyn Lawrence, the staff of The Phillips Collection, and the staffs of the various manuscript collections cited in these notes, especially Esme Bahn and Helen Rutt, Alain L. Locke Papers; Elaine Felsher, Time, Inc., Archives; Victoria Garvin, Museum of Modern Art, Department of Painting and Sculpture; Beth M. Howse and Ann Allen Shockley, Rosenwald Fund Collection; and Rona Roob, Museum of Modern Art Archives.

1. I have written more about Halpert, her gallery, and related topics in my dissertation, "Edith Gregor Halpert and the Downtown Gallery Downtown (1926–1940): A Study in American Art Patronage," University of Michigan, 1989. I am refining and expanding this work into a book, *Inside the Downtown Gallery: A Biography of Edith Gregor Halpert*.

2. Alain Locke, *The Negro in Art: A Pictorial Record of the Negro Artist and of the Negro Theme in Art* (Washington, D.C.: Associates in Negro Folk Education, 1940). It seems likely that the final eight illustrations in part 1, "The Negro as Artist," from Lawrence's *Toussaint L'Ouverture* series (127–29), escaped Halpert's eye. A summary biography of Lawrence appears on p. 133.

3. Halpert to Locke, June 9, 1941, Alain L. Locke Papers, Moorland-Spingarn Research Center, Howard University, Washington, D.C. (hereafter Locke Papers). For more about Locke and his writings about art, see Jeffrey C. Stewart's essay, "(Un)Locke(ing) Jacob Lawrence's *Migration* Series," in this catalogue and Stewart, ed., *The Critical Temper of Alain Locke: A Selection of His Essays on Art and Culture* (New York: Garland Publishing, 1982). Conversations with Stewart have brought me closer to an understanding of Locke's complex aesthetic ideas.

The six-month period (June to December) in which Halpert planned this large and historical exhibition was the longest interval the gallery had taken to prepare an exhibition.

4. Press release, Downtown Gallery, December 2, 1941.

5. Abby Aldrich Rockefeller purchased one of Woodruff's watercolors from Halpert and sent money through Halpert to aid Woodruff. For the interracial cultural climate, see David Levering Lewis, "The New Negro: 1920–1935," *Prospects: An Annual of American Cultural Studies* 3 (1971): 250–70. For Woodruff, see Mary Schmidt Campbell, *Hale Woodruff: 50 Years of His Art* (New York: Studio Museum in Harlem, 1979). Information about Halpert, Rockefeller, Woodruff, and

Locke was gleaned from twenty letters in the Downtown Gallery Papers, Archives of American Art, Smithsonian Institution, Washington, D.C. (hereafter Downtown Gallery Papers) and from a questionnaire I sent to Woodruff and a telephone interview I had with him in January 1978.

6. I have seen nothing in the extant Downtown Gallery Papers or the Locke Papers to indicate that Locke was compensated for his services or expenses when working on the exhibition. However, the financial records of the Downtown Gallery remain closed. Locke never had a grant from the Julius Rosenwald Fund or the Harmon Foundation. In an era before grants from public agencies, he would have had to rely on informal private grants. He was no longer in contact with Charlotte Moser, his previous private patron.

7. See Ellen Harkins Wheat, *Jacob Lawrence: American Painter* (Seattle: University of Washington Press and Seattle Art Museum, 1986), 202–5, 221–23. Additional exhibitions are listed in Locke, *Negro in Art*, 133. The Columbia University exhibition was noted in "Life of Toussaint," *Art Digest*, December 15, 1940, 12.

8. Madelyn Matz of the Division of Motion Pictures, Library of Congress, and a colleague and devoted admirer of Leyda assembled many of Leyda's obituaries for me. They attest to the breadth of his accomplishments in film and American cultural history but do not hint at his role as a mentor to young African American artists. Lawrence recalled Leyda's early support of his work at the planning sessions for this exhibition on June 3, 1992, and January 15, 1993. Although Lawrence remembers seeing the work of von Stroheim, he did not recall the powerful and suggestive narratives of Sergei Eisenstein, with whom Leyda had worked.

Wendy Jeffers, working on a biography of Dorothy Miller and Holger Cahill, brought to my attention that when Leyda was eking out a precarious existence as an independent filmmaker during the early 1930s, he occasionally sold folk art to Halpert's American Folk Art Gallery. Leyda's March 26, 1940, request to Holger Cahill on Museum of Modern Art Film Library Memo stock and a carbon copy of Dorothy Miller's March 27, 1940, recommendation to the Rosenwald Fund are in the Department of Painting and Sculpture Object Files, Museum of Modern Art, New York. Jeffers explained to me that Miller's restrained letter in support of Lawrence was characteristic, especially when Miller wrote about artists who did figurative work rather than abstraction.

9. Lawrence's Rosenwald fellowship materials are held in the Rosenwald Fund Collection, Special Collections, Fisk University Library, Nashville, Tenn. (hereafter Rosenwald Fund Collection). His application includes statements by Lincoln Kirstein; Carl Zigrosser, director of the Weyhe Gallery; Helen Grayson, designer and advisor to the federal theater costume workshop; Charles R. Rogers, director of the Baltimore Museum of Art; Locke; and Dorothy Miller.

Rosenwald (1862–1932) was a first-generation German Jewish merchant from Springfield, Illinois, who rose from local clothier to president and chairman of the board of Sears, Roebuck, & Company. After meeting Booker T. Washington in 1911, he had crusaded for the betterment of Negro education. The Rosenwald Fund established more than 5,000 schools for African Americans in the South using matching funds from the community; supported African American higher education; and acted on its founder's belief that progress depends largely on individual leadership. Rosenwald was one of a small but influential group of Jewish philanthropists who rigorously supported the welfare and rights of African Americans.

I learned about Rosenwald and the fund he established from: Julius Rosenwald, "Principles of Public Giving," *Atlantic Monthly*, May 1929, 599–606; "Rosenwald Dead; Nation Mourns Him," *New York Times*, January 7, 1932, 1, 18; Edwin R. Embree and Julia Waxman, *Investment in People: The Story of the Julius Rosenwald Fund* (New York: Harper and Bros., 1949), 5–27, 31–33, 143–55, 238–61 (list of fellows); and Hasia Diner, *In the Almost Promised Land: American*

Jews and Blacks, 1915–1935 (Westport, Conn.: Greenwood Press, 1977), 166–76, 192 ff. Discussions with Diner about the activities of German-American Jewish philanthropists have helped me better formulate my ideas about Halpert. I believe that Halpert, by mounting a major public exhibition corrective to racism, was consciously or unconsciously declaring how American she had become.

10. Elaine Felsher of the Time, Inc., Archives provided information about Calkins and Francis E. Brennan, *Fortune*'s art director in 1941, as well as about *Fortune*'s editorial process. Correspondence between Halpert and Calkins is in the Downtown Gallery Papers. A July 1, 1941, letter from Calkins to Lawrence is in the Jacob Lawrence Papers, Syracuse University Library Special Collections Department, Syracuse, N.Y. (microfilm in the Archives of American Art, Smithsonian Institution, Washington, D.C.). Correspondence between Locke and Calkins about Locke's advice for the text is in the Locke Papers. For Sheeler, see Carol Troyen and Erica Hirschler, *Charles Sheeler: Paintings and Drawings* (Boston: Museum of Fine Arts, 1987), 162–77.

Halpert and Calkins continued their collaboration, with other Downtown Gallery artists later making art for *Fortune*. *Fortune* commissioned Lawrence to paint *African Gold Rush* for the October 1946 cover (original in the Hirshhorn Museum and Sculpture Garden, Smithsonian Institution) and sent him to the South the following June and July to make ten paintings for the unpublished series "In the heart of the black belt."

11. A telegram from Halpert to Locke in the Locke Papers reads: "PLEASE PHONE MRS CALKINS FORTUNE AT ONCE CAN YOU JOIN ME WEDNESDAY AFTERNOON AT ART CENTER." Halpert and Calkins would have been familiar with the thriving WPA center at the corner of 125th Street and Lenox Avenue near Lawrence's studio. Halpert and Locke both understood that the *Migration* series should be seen before its message might be obscured by the new war (Halpert to Locke, July 1, 1941, Locke Papers).

12. Calkins to Locke, August 28, 1941, Locke Papers; Locke to Calkins, September 4, 1941, Locke Papers. Locke, *The Negro in America* (Chicago: American Library Association, 1933).

13. Lawrence to Halpert, n.d. [October 1941], Downtown Gallery Papers. Lawrence later authorized Halpert to set his prices.

14. Lawrence to Halpert, n.d. [annotated in Halpert's hand, "Nov/1941"], Downtown Gallery Papers.

15. Peter Pollack to Locke, July 25, 1941, Locke Papers. A series of spirited letters between Pollack and Locke (in Pollack's file in the Locke Papers) detail the saga of the Mc Millen and Downtown Gallery exhibitions and comment on Halpert's activities. Pollack tells Locke about the Mc Millen representatives' visits to Chicago to see local artists.

16. "Art by Negroes," *Art Digest*, October 15, 1941, 11, 23.

17. Halpert to Lawrence, November 8, 1941, Downtown Gallery Papers. In the *New York Times*, Howard Devree praised the paintings for their directness, simplicity, imagination, and obvious conviction (November 9, 1941, 1, 10).

18. The other members of the sponsorship committee were Mrs. Ernest R. (Lillian Anderson) Alexander, social worker and member of the NAACP board of directors; Mrs. Francis (Katherine Chapin) Biddle, poet; Mrs. W. Murray (Josephine Boardman) Crane, member of the founding committee of The Museum of Modern Art; Countee Cullen, poet of the Harlem Renaissance; Raymond B. Fosdick, former undersecretary of the League of Nations and president of the Rockefeller Foundation; William C. Handy, jazz trumpeter and composer; Mrs. William E. (Katherine Griffiths) Harmon, widow of the founder and member of the board of the Harmon Foundation; Roland Hayes, concert tenor; Mrs. James Weldon (Grace Nail) Johnson, widow of the poet, teacher, and diplomat; Dr. Malcolm S. Maclean; Archibald MacLeish, poet and Librarian of Congress; Dorothy Maynor, soprano and founder of Harlem School of the Arts; Mrs. Henry (Elinor Fatman) Morgenthau, Jr., activist wife of the secretary of the treasury; Paul Robeson, singer,

actor, and activist; and Ethel Waters, blues singer and stage and film actress. In addition to Locke and Allen, members of the Coordination Committee were Robert Carlen, Carlen Galleries, Horace Pippin's Philadelphia dealer; the Harmon Foundation; Richard Foster Howard, director, Dallas Art Museum; Peter Pollack, South Side Art Center; and Daniel Catton Rich, director, Art Institute of Chicago.

19. Exhibition brochure, "American Negro Art," December 1941, Downtown Gallery Papers.

20. The Newark Museum recently recognized the Harmon Foundation with an exhibition; see Gary Reynolds and Beryl J. Wright, *Against the Odds: African-American Artists and the Harmon Foundation* (Newark, N.J.: Newark Museum, 1989), especially David Driskell, "Mary Beattie Brady and the Administration of the Harmon Foundation," 59–69.

Brady placed Lawrence's *Toussaint L'Ouverture* series at Fisk University; it is now in the Amistad Research Center's Aaron Douglas Collection, New Orleans. She stored the *Frederick Douglass* and *Harriet Tubman* series, supplied the portrait photograph of Lawrence that appeared in *Fortune*, ordered and circulated offprints of the *Fortune* portfolio, and sent copies to Lawrence in New Orleans together with four Downtown Gallery installation photographs. Lawrence to Locke, n.d. [probably January 1942], Locke Papers.

The Downtown Gallery installation photographs are with the Harmon Foundation Photographs, Still Picture Branch, National Archives, Washington, D.C.

21. See Catlett's cogent discussion of the *Migration* series, "Artist with a Message," *People's Voice*, October 21, 1944, clipping in Museum of Modern Art Archives, Public Information Scrapbook, New York. For further discussion of Catlett's criticism, see Patricia Hills, "Jacob Lawrence's *Migration* Series: Weavings of Pictures and Texts," in this catalogue.

22. Halpert to Mrs. Adele M. Levy, January 17, 1941, Downtown Gallery Papers. For more about Levy, see "Mrs. David M. Levy Dead at 67," *New York Times*, March 13, 1960, 86, and *The Mrs. Adele R. Levy Collection: A Memorial Exhibition* (New York: Museum of Modern Art, 1961).

23. Barr to Levy, March 7, 1942, Barr Papers. It is not surprising that Barr and Levy focused on this stark, very abstract panel. At that time The Museum of Modern Art considered abstraction the embodiment of modernism.

24. Halpert to Duncan Phillips, February 5, 1942, and to Mrs. Duncan Phillips, February 21, 1942, Downtown Gallery Papers.

25. Both statements are found in Museum of Modern Art Archives, Department of Circulating Exhibitions, New York.

26. Lawrence to Locke, n.d. [1938 or 1939], Locke Papers.

27. Lawrence, interview with Carroll Greene, October 26, 1968, Archives of American Art, Smithsonian Institution, Washington, D.C., 24, 64.

Lawrence would repeatedly experience the results of Halpert's extraordinary efforts on behalf of her artists. During the war she used her connections and her persistence to secure special assignments for Lawrence and other Downtown Gallery artists in uniform. When he suffered a mental breakdown in 1949, Halpert enlisted her long-time friend Dr. Nathaniel Uhr, then at the Menninger Clinic in Topeka, Kansas, in her search for the best treatment plan and facility. She then willingly contributed to his medical expenses and found a job for his wife.

In 1953, without being consulted, Lawrence and the other artists who had come to the Downtown Gallery after 1936 were abruptly transferred to the newly opened Charles Alan Gallery as part of a settlement between Halpert and Alan, her long-time associate. Halpert maintained her loyalty to Lawrence and her devotion to his work and retained at least three major paintings in her personal collection: *At the Piano*, *Drama—Halloween Party*, and *Fantasy* (*The Edith G. Halpert Collection of American Paintings* [New York: Sotheby Parke Bernet, 1973], nos. 174, 184, 199).

Jacob Lawrence in his Coast Guard uniform with two children at the Museum of Modern Art exhibition of the *Migration* series, 1944 (International News)

Jacob Lawrence's *Migration* Series: Weavings of Pictures and Texts

PATRICIA HILLS

When Jacob Lawrence finished his *Migration* series in 1941, he had created a new theme for the twentieth century—an imaginative, yet didactic, pictorial narrative representing the great migration of African Americans from the South to the industrial cities of the North beginning during World War I. Within his grand, ambitious story, Lawrence incorporated scenes of labor, of the regional landscape, and of families interacting in their daily routines and embarking on a journey that would irrevocably change the country and themselves. What he accomplished was a weaving of sixty pictures and sixty text captions that draws the viewer through time and geography, struggle and hope. Like a West African *griot* (a "professional . . . praise singer and teller of accounts") Lawrence spun a tale of the past that had relevance for the present and the future.[1]

The completed series won acceptance from the start. It was obvious that the twenty-three-year-old artist had a special gift for communicating a great epic of American history in dynamic modernist terms. The influential cultural writer Alain Locke brought Lawrence to the attention of art dealer Edith Halpert. She, in turn, arranged for *Fortune* magazine to reproduce a substantial number of the panels (twenty-six in all) in color in the November 1941 issue, and she showed the series at her Downtown Gallery in December 1941.[2] Halpert did not need to persuade Duncan Phillips and Alfred H. Barr, Jr., director of The Museum of Modern Art, of the worth of the series; they already were vying for them and ended by each acquiring half.[3] All sixty panels then toured the country for two years and returned to New York in October 1944 for a homecoming exhibition at the Modern, which also displayed Lawrence's genre scenes of Coast Guard life.[4]

The 1944 exhibition elicited the most extensive press coverage of Lawrence's work to date, with critics praising both his unique modernist style and his choice of subject. Emily Genauer wrote in the *New York World-Telegram and Sun* that she liked Lawrence's modern style, his "splendid gift for color and design, integrating both into compositions distinguished by their highly sophisticated treatment of blocky, almost primitive forms."[5] The reviewer for the *Art Digest*, on the other hand, focused on his theme of the relocation of African Americans "in large quantities into the war plants of the urban industrial North at a time of national crisis"—a time similar to his own—and observed that "no professional sociologist could have stated the case with more clarity—or dignity."[6]

Artist Elizabeth Catlett spoke for the African American community when she wrote in the *People's Voice*:

> One cannot look at these seemingly simple portrayals of the startling lack of the bare necessities of life, the frustrations and complexities of daily struggle, and the determined mass movement towards democratic equality of these Negroes without a decided self examination.[7]

To Catlett, however, the artistic achievement rested on his successful alloy of subject and style. The young artist was already "one of America's truly great painters," because "his style of painting with almost elemental color and design is a perfect means for the expression of the fundamental needs of the Negro. . . . He strips his material to the bone."[8]

In *Art News*, Aline Loucheim agreed that Lawrence's modernist style went beyond notions of pure painting:

> The way Lawrence sees is in terms of pattern in bright primary color, unmodulated . . . and in simplification of form. Form is simplified in order to articulate the essentials. Detail is suppressed except where it functions both as part of design and basic part of fact. His steep perspective generates immediacy.[9]

Installation view of the *Migration* series, exhibited at The Museum of Modern Art, New York, October 10–November 5, 1944. The exhibition included all sixty panels (photograph courtesy of The Museum of Modern Art, New York).

These critics recognized that Lawrence had forged a modernism—clarity of form, reductive color range, absence of tonal variations, and simplified spatial relations—that expressed deeply felt social concerns.

That these voices should blend into a rousing chorus of admiration for the *Migration* series is not difficult to understand. Whether consciously or not, Lawrence had his hand on the pulse of America in early 1940 when he first proposed the series to the Julius Rosenwald Fund as a project worthy of a fellowship. For different, but often overlapping, reasons a wide audience was in place to respond—African American cultural nationalists, left-radical artists, capitalist business executives, and white liberals.

From the people of his own community Lawrence acquired the mantle of storyteller to spin out the saga of the descendants of Africa in the American continent. During his Harlem youth, he attended after-school classes at Utopia House and learned about African American history; he remembered particularly a Mr. Allen telling about Toussaint L'Ouverture.[10] He also recalled going to meetings when he was older, at which a "Professor" Seyfert lectured on black history. Lawrence recalls that Seyfert wanted "to get black artists and young people such as myself who were interested in art . . . to select as our content black history. . . . For me, and for a few others, Seyfert was a most inspiring and exciting man, in that he helped to give us something that we needed at the time."[11] When Lawrence embarked on his series of the lives of Toussaint L'Ouverture, Frederick Douglass, and Harriet Tubman, he was taking on the role of community *griot*, and he received encouragement for his efforts from such cultural figures as Alain Locke.

Left-radical artists also urged the telling of African American history and encouraged the artistic expression of the conflicts, struggles, and victories of the socially and economically oppressed.[12] These radicals were in the forefront of protests against the trial of the Scottsboro Boys and agitated for antilynching legislation debated in Congress in the mid-1930s.[13] Many of them taught at the American Artists School, which Lawrence attended from 1936 to 1938,[14] and they included such activists and artist-theorists as Harry Gottlieb, Louis Lozowick, and Anton Refregier.

The ideas of the radicals must be incorporated into any assessment of the influences operating on young Lawrence at this time.[15] The school advertised an innovative curriculum that included "weekly lectures by recognized authorities" that would "provide the student with an historical approach to his creative problems." The purpose was to give the student "an understanding of modern society itself, its forces, tendencies, and conflicts which can only serve to deepen his aesthetic outlook and capacities."[16] To these artists, art had a social purpose.

At the other end of the political spectrum, within the business world a receptive audience was being developed for imagery of African Americans coming north to work in industry. Publisher Henry Luce presented to the readers of his *Fortune* magazine a full-color spread of almost half of the *Migration* series in the November 1941 issue, when the nation was gearing up for war production.[17] Luce's often-quoted "American Century" essay, published in the February 17, 1941, issue of *Life*, projected an ideal of the United States as an international economic leader and humanitarian provider for the entire world. But, warned Luce, this "will not happen unless our vision of America as a world power includes a passionate devotion to great American ideals . . . a love of freedom, a feeling for the equality of opportunity, a tradition of self-reliance and independence and also of co-operation."[18]

To Luce and others, the image of the racially integrated factory would be a necessary step toward that vision of equality of opportunity. The image was needed immediately; the reality could come later. The picture magazines of 1941 were filled with positive, almost propagandistic, images of American industry, running efficiently and conflict-free, and the August and November issues of *The Crisis*, the journal of the National Association for the Advancement of Colored People, ran stories on training programs for blacks in the defense industry.[19] Thus, to the Luce editors, Lawrence's pictures could be seen as a first step—images heralding the

inevitability of African Americans in the work force and cautioning against the continuation of racism.

Progressive liberals, many connected with New Deal programs and involved with organizations like the Rosenwald Fund, would not disagree with the *Fortune* crowd, nor even with the left radicals' political outlook in the early 1940s. They would, however, be especially drawn to themes of social uplift, of advancement through hard work and education. Thus the directors of the Rosenwald Fund may have been predisposed toward Lawrence's 1940 grant proposal. He had the credentials, and he already had a successful track record of painting historical series of African American life, such as the *Toussaint L'Ouverture* series (1937–38) of forty-one panels, *Frederick Douglass* (1938–39) of thirty-two panels, and *Harriet Tubman* (1939–40) of thirty-one panels. As he completed each series his reputation

The CRISIS November, 1941 • Fifteen Cents

TRAINING FOR DEFENSE
Hampton Shop Student

Training for Defense, cover of *The Crisis*, November 1941

grew, so that he felt confident enough to list as his references Lincoln Kirstein, Alain Locke, and the director of the Baltimore Museum of Art, Charles Rogers.

Their recommendations glow with admiration and provide proof that Lawrence had already developed a following among the cognoscenti. Kirstein, for example, recommended Lawrence as

> the most capable negro artist whose work I have ever had the opportunity to look at. His series of paintings seem to me strikingly original, and possessed of great inherent beauty. Unlike so many others, he is not imitative, but has a genuine emotion, and is extraordinarily successful in conveying it. I feel absolutely certain that with the necessary encouragement and slight security, he could be the most important negro artist this country has yet produced.[20]

Rogers, who had mounted a major exhibition of contemporary African American art for the Baltimore Museum that included Lawrence's *Toussaint* series, praised the artist as "undoubtedly the most talented, sincere and creative" of African American artists.[21]

Locke, who knew Lawrence's art most intimately, called the *Toussaint* series "the sensation" of the Baltimore Museum's exhibition:

> What impresses me about Lawrence is his ability to combine social interest and interpretation . . . with a straight art approach. . . . There is little or no hint of social propaganda in his pictures, and no slighting of the artistic problems involved, such as one finds in many of the contemporary social-theme painters. Yet his work has a stirring social and racial appeal.

Locke's recommendation also speaks of Lawrence's artistic development and praises the "considerable growth in maturity and power" of his compositions.[22]

Indeed, by the *Tubman* series, done a year after *Douglass* and probably not yet seen by Locke, Lawrence had reached his full powers as a pictorial *griot*. His link to his community's storytelling traditions comes through not just in the subject matter of the *Tubman* series—the story of a heroic woman's journey from slavery to freedom and her subsequent rescue of other slaves—but in the telling of the story through the twin means of extended captions and

colorful pictures. Lawrence learned from *Tubman* to work with the rhythms of both words and images.

The captions for *Harriet Tubman*, when read as a continuous narrative, recall the conventions of slave narratives: the need to frame the story with testimonials by white writers, the significance of the journey as a metaphorical and Biblical testing of faith, and the importance of the slave's metamorphosis into a man or woman with an identity and a voice. In this series, the collective yearnings and hopes of the people coalesce in the story and voice of one individual.

But Lawrence's development into a master artist is most apparent in his pictorial construction of the *Tubman* series. The thirty-one panels form groups of four to six panels, within which are rhythms, contrasts, and closures. Vertical panels create a syncopation with horizontal ones; scenes of crowded all-over forms zoom to single, iconic images; bright day scenes are preceded or followed by night scenes; indoor scenes contrast with outdoor ones; and angular, diagonal movements shift to rounded and calm forms.[23]

In 1940 Lawrence was ready to begin a more ambitious series. His conceptual powers had matured, and he had full control over his techniques. He knew his *Migration* series would involve a more complicated orchestration in order to represent by pictures not just the phenomenon of people on the move but also the underlying economic and social forces.[24]

In his application to the Rosenwald Fund, Lawrence outlined the plan of the narrative into eight sections: "Causes of the Migration"; "Stimulation of the Migration"; "The Spread of the Migration"; "The Efforts to Check the Migration"; "Public Opinion Regarding the Migration"; "The Effects of the Migration on the South"; "The Effects of the Migration on Various Parts of the North"; and "The Effects of the Migration on the Negro."

Although Lawrence wrote in his application that he had not yet begun the *Migration* project, he had at least studied Emmett J. Scott's *Negro Migration During the War*, first published in 1920. Six of his sections are exact quotations from Scott's chapter headings. Moreover, in his listing of subheadings, Lawrence follows the development of Scott's analysis, except that the artist tends to give a positive spin to his topics. For example, Lawrence lists "the prevalence of mob violence" as a cause of the migration, but he does not mention lynching, which Scott discusses. Lawrence no doubt wished to prevent his liberal supporters from worrying that he might launch into the propaganda that Locke had so carefully assured them he would avoid. Other examples of Lawrence's positive outlook come in the section devoted to "The Effects of the Migration on the South." He mentions that wages for Negroes increased by 150 percent, but Scott states a more conservative 100 percent at the most.[25] While Lawrence says that "labor unions opened their doors to Negroes," Scott had declared, "the trade unions have been compelled to yield, although complete economic freedom of the negro in the South is still a matter of prospect."[26] Lawrence makes another point—"Business decreases to such an extent as to cause the closing of shops"—that Scott did not discuss.[27] These variations indicate that Lawrence felt free to appropriate facts from other sources, but he felt no compunction to follow these sources doggedly.

Lawrence's last section, "The Effects of the Migration on the Negro," is not based on Scott's chapter headings, but is drawn instead from the collective experience of the artist's own community. The theme had a personal dimension as well: his own parents had come from the South looking for better working and living conditions. His mother, a domestic worker from Virginia, met his father, a cook from South Carolina, in Atlantic City, and Lawrence was born there. When his parents separated some time later, his mother took Lawrence and his sister and brother to Philadelphia. Later, when Lawrence was about thirteen, she moved the children to Harlem,[28] where they met others who recounted their own stories of the migration. Thus, even though he looked at Scott's book and later went to the New York Public Library's Schomburg Collection, the planning and execution of the *Migration* series came as much from his own emotional and social experience as from books.[29] To Lawrence, the telling of the story needed to incorporate that experience.

To elaborate that point, Lawrence ended his "Plan of Work" with a statement that the significance of the project rested "on its educational value." He argued that since the Great Migration had an impact on the entire nation, African Americans should realize their contribution to history, and others should know it as well.[30] Collective pride in past achievements would help stimulate individual feelings of self-worth in the present. Lawrence well understood the psychological reasoning of August Wilson, who said much

later: "The real struggle, since the African first set foot on the continent, is the affirmation of the value of oneself."[31]

But besides the individual, psychological benefits, Lawrence believed that reminders of historical gains would spur collective action toward securing better social and economic conditions for the whole community. He felt that artists could make a difference by visualizing inspiring themes, just as the *griot* can verbalize hopes in the most ordinary of us. In a statement for the Harmon Foundation in 1940, Lawrence declared the agenda behind the *Toussaint L'Ouverture* series:

I didn't do it as a historical thing, but because I believe these things tie up the Negro today. We don't have a

Russell Lee. Church service, Illinois, ca. 1941. Published in Edwin Rosskam and Richard Wright, *Twelve Million Black Voices*, 1941, and selected by The Museum of Modern Art for the wall text for its installation of the *Migration* series in 1944 (Library of Congress, Farm Security Administration Collection)

Cottonfield workers with bags, from Pare Lorentz's film *The River*, 1936–37 (National Archives, Farm Security Administration Collection)

physical slavery, but an economic slavery. If these people, who were so much worse off than the people today could conquer their slavery, we certainly can do the same thing.[32]

The Migration of the Negro differs from Lawrence's earlier series by singling out no one hero or heroine; the protagonists are just folks, like his parents. There is not even a skin-color differentiation, which might have connoted class differences; gender differences are also minimized.[33] The people as a whole—acting with a collective will—take on a heroic dimension beyond distinctions of class or gender. Unlike the diaspora of the Middle Passage—when some fifteen to twenty million Africans were forced to cross the Atlantic as slaves for the New World plantations—African Americans leaving the South during and after World War I were acting as free agents.[34] Their struggles together—each moving north on his or her own initiative as well as helping each other—ought to revolutionize, Lawrence believed, the

consciousness of all African Americans in the early 1940s.

The visual culture of the 1930s stimulated young Lawrence. He was long familiar with photographic essays such as those published in *Life* and other magazines. Several photographic books of the time also contributed to the visual culture of social concern. Margaret Bourke-White and Erskine Caldwell's *You Have Seen Their Faces* (1937), Dorothea Lange and Paul Taylor's *An American Exodus* (1938), and, later, Walker Evans and James Agee's *Let Us Now Praise Famous Men* (1941) all focused on the people, both black and white, rooted to the soil of the rural South.

Of all the photographic documentary books, the one that comes closest to Lawrence's project was Edwin Rosskam's *Twelve Million Black Voices* (1941), which included a long text by Richard Wright. Rosskam borrowed almost 150 archival photographs of African Americans by Dorothea Lange, Jack Delano, Russell Lee, Arthur Rothstein, Ben Shahn, and Marion Post Wolcott that these photographers had made on assignment for the Farm Security Administration in the 1930s. The project was advancing at the very time that Lawrence was working on his own pictures, and Wright's text could well have applied to Lawrence's series:

This text, while purporting to render a broad picture of the processes of Negro life in the United States, intentionally does not include in its considerations those areas of Negro life which comprise the so-called 'talented tenth' . . . . Their exclusion from these pages does not imply any invidious judgment, nor does it stem from any desire to underestimate their progress and contributions; they are omitted in an effort to simplify a depiction of a complex movement of a debased feudal folk toward a twentieth-century urbanization.[35]

Lawrence's project also aimed to depict the rural working classes of black America rather than elite social groupings. In a statement titled "My Opinion About Painting," published in the mid-1940s, he concluded: "My pictures express my life and experiences. I paint the things I know about and the things I have experienced. The things I have experienced extend into my national, racial and class group. So I paint the American Negro working class."[36]

Lawrence developed as a *griot* at a time when storytelling was an aesthetic strategy in the general culture of the visual arts. We have already mentioned photographic books. Documentary filmmakers also turned to storytelling techniques to reach a mass audience. In many respects, the closest analogue to Lawrence's *Migration* series is provided by the documentary films of the 1930s, particularly Pare Lorentz's *The River*, shot during 1936 and 1937 under the auspices of the Farm Security Administration to publicize the government's land reclamation programs.[37] With a musical score by Virgil Thomson and a prose-poem script, Lorentz retells the story of the annual spring rising of the great North American rivers that flood the land in the valleys and flow on toward the Gulf of Mexico. The narration turns tragic when it dwells on soil erosion brought on by human ignorance and poverty, but it ends with a burst of enthusiasm for the harnessing of natural power made possible by government agencies such as the Tennessee Valley Authority and the Civilian Conservation Corps. Both the *Migration* and Lorentz's *The River* deliver messages of hope after explicating historical circumstances. Both communicate through such artistic devices as repetition, movement, synecdoche (the use of the fragment or partial view to represent the whole), and abrupt juxtapositions of images.[38] And both weave together

Man sitting on wheelbarrow, from Pare Lorentz's film *The River*, 1936–37 (National Archives, Farm Security Administration Collection)

Man with lantern, from Pare Lorentz's film *The River*, 1936–37 (National Archives, Farm Security Administration Collection)

images and words, which at times enhance one another's messages, but which often develop as independent constructions of meaning.

Lawrence crafted his text in plain, schoolbook English. By the time he wrote the captions for the panels from his research notes in March 1941, he had looked at written sources other than Scott's *Negro Migration During the War.* Carter G. Woodson's *A Century of Negro Migration,* published in 1918, seems to have been another source. Lawrence's language never exactly matches that of the two scholars, since he was writing captions rather than discursive prose. Instead—coming as much from the oral tradition as from scholarship—it sounds like spoken words.[39]

While Lawrence makes many of the same points as Scott and Woodson, he differs by stressing at the outset that World War I caused the labor shortage, which in turn spurred migration to the northern cities. Not until panel 8 does he mention the other causes that Scott and Woodson had advanced along with the labor shortage theory: the floods of 1915, boll weevil damage to the crops in 1915 and 1916, and the low wages that African Americans had to endure.[40] And not until panels 14 and 15—a quarter of the way into his story—does he tackle discrimination in the courts and lynchings as motives for migration. In contrast, he had placed those issues at the very beginning of his list of subjects in his Rosenwald Fund "Plan of Work." By 1941, however, the preoccupations of most Americans had shifted. Especially to Lawrence, who had never lived in the South and who most likely was seeing photographs of defense production in the current periodicals, World War I with its increased economic opportunities for African Americans must have loomed as the primary cause for the migration.

Although Lawrence's text conveys facts, he arranges it to evoke a mood. We hear three voices—each coming from a different sociological geography—intoning facts about the momentum of the migration, the promises and the hardships of the North, the poverty and racism of the South. He ends with a poetic coda that affirms both that they will prevail and that the cycle will be renewed: "And the migrants kept coming."

The pictures set up rhythms for interpretative analysis that parallel those of the text. As we walk from panel to panel, our attention continually shifts to absorb new images and

new possible meanings. However, we are always free to return to or glance back at previous images, which we cannot do when experiencing the diachronic progression of film. The encounter with Lawrence's *Migration* is thus both kinesthetic and dialectical, with newer interpretations superseding earlier ones, but never rigidly, as we move through space to view the series.

Lawrence's first panel—"During the World War there was a great migration North by Southern Negroes"—shows a crowd of figures pushing their way through gates marked "Chicago," "New York," and "St. Louis."[41] The flat shapes and latticework of the station architecture control the movement of the figures. The dark turquoise, rose, brown, and black shapes that are the people stream toward the openings that represent the passageways to the cities.

The caption for the second panel highlights the labor shortages in the North: "The World War had caused a great shortage in Northern industry and also citizens of foreign countries were returning home." The picture shows a solitary white workman driving a steamshovel. The sequence of the first three panels leads us to read the captions as images of effects (panel 1), causes (panel 2), and effects (panel 3). This third panel, with its flying wedge of people moving left against a backdrop of migrating birds, quickens the pace of the migrants.[42]

The fourth panel repeats the single-figure motif, but here Lawrence introduces the African American laborer—a muscular man holding a hammer over his head. The caption reads, "The Negro was the largest source of labor to be found after all others had been exhausted." Lawrence notes the class differences between the African American and his white counterpart. The white man is a skilled worker driving a vehicle; he has a face and features. The black man, on the other hand, is a common laborer whose face is obscured by his muscular arm.[43] Hence, a new reading develops based on the pictures as a foursome, independent of the captions: movement, the white worker, movement, the black worker.

And yet this interpretation shifts with the fifth panel—the partial view of the railroad locomotive with its headlights ablaze, black smoke pouring from its stack and its bell ringing. Suddenly, the large spike the black worker is poised to hit suggests a railroad scene, despite the indoor setting, and he is transformed into the folk hero John Henry, "the railroading man."

Russell Lee. Tenements, South Side Chicago. Published in Edwin Rosskam and Richard Wright, *Twelve Million Black Voices*, 1941, and selected by The Museum of Modern Art for the wall text for its installation of the *Migration* series in 1944 (Library of Congress, Farm Security Administration Collection)

The sixth and seventh panels (the view of the inside of the train with its sleeping passengers and the view from inside the window to the outside fields whizzing by)[44] lead us to conclude that Lawrence meant the beginning of the series (panels 1–7) to focus on the railroad as facilitator of the cause and effect process. Because panels 2 and 5 represent vehicles moving to the left, our eyes can trick us into interpreting the white man in the cab as the engineer of a train driving the migrants to the North.

However, we need to return to the words of the captions: panels 7, 8, and 9 indicate that Lawrence is shifting to statements about the southern agricultural economy. We then realize that the seventh panel, instead of being linked to the previous six, belongs visually to the two that follow, which, like it, are vertical and focus on the crops of the countryside. What differs among these three panels is the perspective viewpoint: Panel 7 suggests the moving eye looking out over fluttering ribbons of color that are the fields of crops; panel 8, a fixed eye looking at a poor crop

drowned in a flood of water; panel 9, a fixed eye telescoping in to the cotton bolls where the wretched weevils do their mischief. A rhythmic pattern of horizontal and vertical panels emerges for the first nine paintings: a-a-a; b-a-b; b-b-b. Similar rhythms occur throughout the series, but as improvisations rather than as formulaic patterns.

Panels 10 and 11 introduce the impoverishment of southern families; figures sit or stand in interiors bereft of material possessions and at kitchen tables with meager provisions. Poor living conditions, Lawrence tells us, led to increased migration: hence, panel 12 returns to a scene of people crowding the ticket windows of a train station.

The migration, until now considered the effect of economic causes, becomes itself a cause for further economic deterioration in panel 13: "Due to the South's losing so much of its labor, the crops were left to dry and spoil." From here to the end of the series, we clearly understand that the migration and the economic and social conditions mutually and reciprocally affect each other.

Panels 14, 15, and 16 form a unit that addresses the issue of southern justice from an African American's point of view. The pattern is interior, exterior, interior; vertical, horizontal, vertical. Moreover, the placement of forms in each panel enhances the ensemble of the three panels as a unit. In panel 14, the lamp on the judge's desk swings to the right. In panel 15, the noose for the lynching hangs in the exact middle of the threesome. In panel 16, the grieving woman's body turns toward the left and brings to a close the group as a whole.

Next come panels addressing discrimination that are interspersed with more panels of migration. People work, talk among themselves, go to the railroad station, are harassed by the police, desert their homes. The pace quickens. Each scene is self-contained—a quiltwork patch of form and color—and yet essential to the rhythmic pattern of any given sequence. Art historical quotations and references occur here and there. The figures in panel 24 resemble those of workers painted on the walls of a pharaoh's tomb; panel 25 evokes the contemporary abstract compositions of the 1930s. Thus we move from panel to panel, forming visual interpretations, recollections, and reinterpretations that move along in tandem with the rhetorical development of the text.[45]

Midway through the series, at panel 31, Lawrence paints the first scene of the urban North as seen by the arriving migrants: a flat wall of building fronts punctuated by both open and shaded windows, a metaphor for the city where openings of opportunity occur in a facade of seeming isolation and indifference. At this point we realize that Lawrence's weave has become a monumental braid of northern, southern, and migration scenes. Like a cornrow braid, where top hairs disappear as nape hairs come into the plait, the southern scenes become fewer as the northern scenes increase.

The next three panels return to the migrants and the South. Increasingly scenes appear that fill out the landscape of the North: the Chicago stockyards (panel 36), steel manufacturing (panel 37), railroad work (panel 38). More scenes follow of the moving migration (panels 39, 40). Then Lawrence shifts again to the South, where measures to keep the migrants from leaving range from terror to appeasement: the labor agent is jailed (panel 41), the police arrest departing migrants (panel 42), and community leaders initiate some reforms to stay the flight of the migrants (panel 43).[46] Unlike the more dynamic migration scenes, these last

Edwin Rosskam. Boy in front of apartment house, Chicago, ca. 1941. Published in Rosskam and Richard Wright, *Twelve Million Black Voices*, 1941, and selected by The Museum of Modern Art for the wall text for its installation of the *Migration* series in 1944 (Library of Congress, Farm Security Administration Collection)

three are all bilaterally symmetrical; their stunning colors and iconic images rivet our thoughts to a social structure basically intolerant of change.

Three-quarters through the series, at panel 45, Lawrence presents the first image of a hopeful, extended family looking out the train window at the industrial North. The next three vertical panels represent crowded living conditions for the migrants in the North—conditions discussed at length in Scott's and Woodson's studies. In panel 48 we see only parts of iron beds with valises tucked under them; the effect of this fragmentary view is to suggest an endless row of beds. Lawrence switches to another narrative device for panel 49 when he presents a literal map of segregated seating in northern restaurants.

Violence erupts in three scenes of race riots, but Lawrence carefully explains, in panel 50, that "many of these riots occurred because the Negro was used as a strike breaker in many of the Northern industries." In other words, racial violence was fomented by the antiunion bosses, not the workers. The next three panels represent the different social conditions migrants experienced, including class discrimination within the urban African American community (panel 53).

Near the end of the series Lawrence takes us briefly back to the South with scenes of the last groups of people to leave—Negro professionals (panel 56) and female workers such as laundresses (panel 57). The two scenes before the final one show children at school (panel 58) and a voting booth (panel 59). To Lawrence, as to W.E.B. Du Bois and others, better educational facilities and the franchise promised African Americans greater self-respect, although the presence of a white policeman with a billy club at the polls and the regimentation of the voters standing rigidly in line suggests that white political control compromises the freedom won with the vote.[47] The last, panel 60, swings back to the horizontal format with dozens of migrants standing by the railroad track waiting for their train, and once again the refrain, "And the migrants kept coming."

Jacob Lawrence's *Migration* series is greater than the sum of its parts. Given his enormous talent and the encouragement he received from major figures in the cultural and artistic worlds, Lawrence was also in the right place at the right time to undertake such an ambitious project. He created a didactic public art, capable of educating and inspiring Americans looking for jobs and a better life in the northern cities and exploring ways to get along with each other. The visual and textual sources were diverse—ranging from documentary photographs to film to New York modernism and from books and pamphlets in the Schomburg Collection to street-corner lectures, poetry readings in Harlem art centers, and political meetings—but the resulting work of art sprang from Lawrence's understanding and intuition about the course of American history. He has, in fact, always held to the philosophy that the "Negro experience" is "the American experience."[48] Through his own art, that belief rings true.

NOTES

I want to thank Elizabeth Hutton Turner and the team of scholars she put together to advise on this exhibition, particularly Henry Louis Gates, Jr., Richard J. Powell, Jeffrey C. Stewart, Diane Tepfer, and Deborah Willis. I am also grateful to the staff at the W.E.B. Du Bois Institute where I was visiting scholar during 1991–92; I want to single out for thanks Professor Gates, Randall K. Burkett, and visiting scholars Amritjit Singh and Robert E. Fox, who advised me at crucial moments. The staffs in the various archives of The Museum of Modern Art, the Schomburg Center for Research in Black Culture of the New York Public Library, and the Syracuse University Library Special Collections Department were particularly helpful. Kevin Whitfield gave the manuscript his usual astute reading. I also want to acknowledge the encouragement of Terry Dintenfass. The many conversations I have had with Gwen and Jake Lawrence in the last decade have helped me understand not only Jake's work but the cultural milieu of African Americans in Harlem.

1. Definition by Jan Vansina, *Oral Tradition as History* (Madison: University of Wisconsin Press, 1985), 37. This West African term has come into street use today.
2. See Jeffrey C. Stewart, "(Un)Locke(ing) Jacob Lawrence's *Migration* Series," and Diane Tepfer, "Edith Gregor Halpert: Impresario of Jacob Lawrence's *Migration* Series," both in this catalogue. See also Ellen Harkins Wheat, *Jacob Lawrence: American Painter* (Seattle: University of Washington Press and Seattle Art Museum, 1986), 60–65, for a discussion of the *Migration* series.
3. The Modern got the even-numbered panels because Mrs. David M. Levy, their donor, liked no. 46. Lawrence wrote to Halpert in October 1941 from New Orleans that he did not want to break up the set "because the complete story was conceived within the sixty paintings therefore to sell any one painting out of the set would make it an incomplete story." Downtown Gallery Papers, Archives of American Art, Smithsonian Institution, Washington, D.C. (hereafter Downtown Gallery Papers). Lawrence agreed to the split when he learned of the two museums involved.
4. According to Wheat, *Lawrence*, 70, the *Coast Guard* series was housed in the Coast Guard Archives and most were subsequently lost. See Wheat, pls. 32 and 33, for reproductions of two of them.
5. Clipping included in Exhibitions Scrapbook, no. 61, Museum of Modern Art Archives, New York City. It was typical for critics at the time to use words such as "primitive" when discussing the art of African Americans.
6. *Art Digest* 19 (November 1, 1944), 7.
7. Catlett's article was titled "Artist with a Message," clipping dated October 21, 1944, Exhibitions Scrapbook, no. 61, Museum of Modern Art Archives, New York City.
8. Ibid.
9. *Art News* (October 15, 1944), 15. Loucheim wrote under the name Aline Saarinen after she married Eero Saarinen.
10. See statement issued by the Harmon Foundation, Inc., dated November 12, 1940, Downtown Gallery Papers.
11. Lawrence to Charles Alan, December 29, 1972, collection the artist; quoted in Wheat, *Lawrence*, 35.
12. Many of these left radicals belonged to the Communist Party, which in the summer of 1935 entered into its Popular Front period. The new policy urged an end to radical sectarianism and encouraged the making of broad alliances with a spectrum of liberal groups, including New Deal Democrats, in the fight against fascism. Although, in general, pictorial themes of revolutionary class struggle began to wane, radical artists in the Popular Front period still produced pictures of bloody strikes and lynchings along with their antifascist pictures.

    The party urged a more balanced view of American history and promoted studies of African American groups and individuals. Mark Naison, *Communists in Harlem during the Depression* (New York: Grove Press, 1984), 214, states: "During the Popular Front era, the Party won the respect of many Harlem leaders through its effort to improve conditions in Harlem schools, to have black history recognized and taught, and to remove racially biased teachers and textbooks."
13. Two antilynching exhibitions were held in New York in 1935. The NAACP organized one that opened at the Jacques Seligmann Galleries on February 16 but closed shortly thereafter. A show sponsored by the John Reed Club, the Artists' Union, and other left activist organizations opened at the A.C.A. Gallery on March 3.
14. Most published chronologies of Lawrence's life—see Wheat, *Lawrence*, and Milton W. Brown, *Jacob Lawrence* (New York: Whitney Museum of American Art, 1974)—give his dates of attendance as 1937 to 1939. However, on his 1940 application to the Rosenwald Fund he states the dates as "1936–1938." He also gives precise dates as to his tenure as "senior artist" on the WPA: "May, 1938, to October, 1939" at the salary of "$1000 per year." In 1939 the WPA instituted a rule dropping

artists from the rolls after eighteen months. The reapplication process was arduous.

15. The school was the continuation of the art school founded in the early 1930s by the New York Chapter of the John Reed Club, an organization started in 1929 by artist members of the Communist Party and their sympathetic friends. When the party shifted to the Popular Front period in the summer of 1935, the John Reed Clubs and all their projects were disbanded as too politically sectarian for the new policy of alliances with liberal groups. The radical artists then regrouped and formed the American Artists School.

16. "American Artists School," *Art Front* 3, no. 7 (October 1937): 19. Lawrence's letter from artist-teacher Sol Wilson dated August 26, 1937, awarding him a scholarship, is affixed to a page of a scrapbook that Lawrence kept during these years, now located in the Jacob Lawrence Papers, Syracuse University Library Special Collections Department (hereafter Lawrence Papers). The other faculty offering classes in the fall of 1937 included Alexander Alland, Emilio Amero, Francis Criss, Robert M. Cronbach, Hilda Deutsch, Tully Filmus, Ruth Gikow, Harry Glassgold, Chaim Gross, John Groth, Charles Hanke, Carl R. Holty, Julian E. Levi, Hugh Miller, Eugene Morley, Anton Refregier, Miron Sokole, Moses Soyer, Nahum Tschacbasov, and Lynd Ward (see Lawrence Papers). Other artists connected to the school included Maurice Glickman, Harry Gottlieb, Louis Lozowick, Elizabeth Olds, Walter Quirt, Philip Reisman, and Raphael Soyer (see Stuart Davis Papers, Archives of American Art, Smithsonian Institution Washington, D.C.). At one time the board of directors included Stuart Davis, William Gropper, Rockwell Kent, Lewis Mumford, Meyer Schapiro, and Max Weber.

We might consider Gottlieb's response to Lawrence to be typical of the faculty's antiracist social values. In a letter postmarked October 4, 1937, and affixed to the aforementioned scrapbook, Gottlieb wrote: "I consider it an honor to have been of any service to you. Not only was I tremendously impressed by your work as an artist, but also knowing the difficulties that the Negro artist is confronted with, I will do what I can to eliminate that unfairness, so that we may all be treated alike you and me, as artists and as human beings." Lawrence gives Gottlieb credit for arranging the scholarship (Lawrence, taped interview with author, July 25, 1983).

17. The twenty-six pictures chosen to be reproduced are: nos. 1, 4, 8, 9, 11, 14, 15, 16, 17, 22, 24, 28, 40, 42, 45, 48, 51, 52, 53, 54, 55, 56, 57, 58, 59, and 60. They include the scenes of the lynching noose (panel 16), the race riot (panel 52), the firebombed building (panel 51), and the southern policeman arresting the migrants (panel 42). The editors of *Fortune* abbreviated many of Lawrence's captions but did not essentially censor his words, except for panel 42 where the caption states that the migrants "were held in the railroad station" rather than, in Lawrence's words, "They . . . arrested the Negroes wholesale."

18. Henry R. Luce, "The American Century," *Life*, February 17, 1941, 63.

19. *Fortune* carried many such articles on defense at this time, as did *The Crisis*. The latter ran pictures of African American soldiers in the 184th and 349th field artillery regiments in the May 1941 issue; in July 1941 it advertised the NAACP conference that had as its theme "The Negro in National Defense." In August *The Crisis* ran an article, "A Call to Negro Youth," about the need for Negro youth in industry, particularly in the defense industry. The cover of the November 1941 issue pictured a young black man working with sheet metal in a Hampton Institute shop. An analysis of the uses and abuses of racism in the workplace introduces problematical issues that cannot be dealt with here.

20. When the United States entered World War II, the Office of War Information sent photographers out on assignment to photograph African Americans working for the war effort; the images often show situations of social integration that did not exist in reality. See Barbara Orbach and Nicholas Natanson, "The Mirror Image: Black Washington

in World War II," *Washington History* 4 (Spring/Summer 1992): 4–25, 92–93.

21. "Confidential Report on Candidate for Fellowship," Julius Rosenwald Fund Collection, Special Collections, Fisk University, Nashville, Tenn. (hereafter Rosenwald Fund Collection). I want to thank Elizabeth Turner for providing me with copies of this archival material.

22. Ibid. The issue of "propaganda" engaged writers in the African American community. W.E.B. Du Bois wrote in his famous article "Criteria of Negro Art" (*The Crisis*, October 1926, 293): "The apostle of Beauty thus becomes the apostle of Truth and Right not by choice but by inner and outer compulsion. Free he is but his freedom is ever bounded by Truth and Justice; and slavery only dogs him when he is denied the right to tell the Truth or recognize an ideal of Justice.

"Thus all Art is propaganda and ever must be, despite the wailing of the purists. I stand in utter shamelessness and say that whatever art I have for writing has been used always for propaganda for gaining the right of black folk to love and enjoy. I do not care a damn for any art that is not used for propaganda. But I do care when propaganda is confined to one side while the other is stripped and silent."

Locke replied to Du Bois in his essay "Art or Propaganda?" *Harlem* 1 (November 1928): 12. "My chief objection to propaganda, apart from its besetting sin of monotony and disproportion, is that it perpetuates the position of group inferiority even in crying out against it. For it believes and speaks under the shadow of a dominant majority whom it harangues, cajoles, threatens or supplicates. It is too extroverted for balance or poise or inner dignity and self-respect. Art in the best sense is rooted in self-expression and whether naive or sophisticated is self-contained. In our spiritual growth genius and talent must more and more choose the role of group expression, or even at times the role of free individualistic expression,—in a word must choose art and put aside propaganda."

23. See Patricia Hills, "Jacob Lawrence as Pictorial Griot: The *Harriet Tubman* Series," *American Art* 7, no. 1 (Winter 1993): 40–59.

24. Articles for *Art Front*, the magazine for the Artists' Union, throughout its years of publication, had urged artists to cope with the underlying causes of economic and social problems. See, for example, Grace Clements, "New Content—New Form," *Art Front*, March 1936, 8–9.

25. Emmett J. Scott, *Negro Migration During the War* (1920; New York: Arno Press, 1969), 86.

26. Ibid., 88.

27. Scott's chapter has its own positive spin in that he hopes that the South will learn from the migration and enact laws and practices to ameliorate the condition of African Americans.

28. See Wheat, *Lawrence*, 250.

29. See Deborah Willis, "The Schomburg Collection: A Rich Resource for Jacob Lawrence," in this catalogue.

30. Lawrence said on his application: "It is important as a part of the evolution of America, since this Migration has affected the whole of America mentally, economically and socially. Since it has had this effect, I feel that my project would lay before the Negroes themselves a little of what part they have played in the History of the United States. In addition, the whole of America might learn some of the history of this particular minority group, of which they know very little" (Lawrence Papers). His proposal included his plan to exhibit the series in schools and public places and to publish it as a book.

31. Quoted in Bill Moyers, *A World of Ideas: Conversations with Thoughtful Men and Women about American Life Today and The Ideas Shaping Our Future* (New York: Doubleday, 1989). I am grateful to Amritjit Singh for bringing this interview to my attention.

32. Statement issued by the Harmon Foundation, Inc., dated November 12, 1940, Downtown Gallery Papers.

33. Other artists of the 1930s made a point to include a variety of skin tones in their pictures of the black community; see the works of

Archibald Motley and William H. Johnson. White radical artists invariably integrated their figure compositions, for example Diego Rivera's *Man at the Crossroads* (destroyed 1934) for Rockefeller Center.

34. Estimates vary from 15–50 million in the period 1482–1888, according to Molefi K. Asante and Mark T. Mattsool, *Historical and Cultural Atlas of African Americans* (New York: Macmillan, 1992), 27.

35. Wright, in Edwin Rosskam and Richard Wright, *Twelve Million Black Voices* (New York: Viking Press, 1941), xix.

36. Clipping, not dated, affixed to Lawrence scrapbook (early years), Lawrence Papers. "ALA News" is inscribed in ink in the margins. I am grateful to Caroline A. Davis, manuscripts librarian, for sending me a photocopy of the clipping.

37. See William Alexander, *Film on the Left: American Documentary Film from 1931 to 1942* (Princeton, N.J.: Princeton University Press, 1981).

38. William Stott, in *Documentary Expression and Thirties America* (New York: Oxford University Press, 1973), 212, credits the documentary film as a major precedent for the documentary book and quotes Alfred Kazin, "who thought Pare Lorentz had developed this 'new genre' in *The River* [1937], the words and images of which were not only mutually indispensable, a kind of commentary upon each other, but curiously interchangeable." Stott then reminds the reader that earlier books such as the *Pittsburgh Survey* (1909–14) were also sources for the documentary photo-text book.

   Lawrence worked in the CCC for six months in 1936 and may well have seen the film after it premiered in 1937. He knew people in film circles, for in 1940 Jay Leyda, then working in the film department of the Museum of Modern Art, introduced Lawrence to Orozco (Lawrence, conversation with the Phillips team of exhibition consultants, January 15, 1993).

39. Unlike his text for *Harriet Tubman*, which came from two literary sources. See Hills, "Lawrence as Pictorial Griot."

40. See Carter G. Woodson, *A Century of Negro Migration* (1918; New York: Russell & Russell, 1969), 168: "What then is the cause? There have been *bulldozing*, terrorism, maltreatment and what not of persecution; but the Negroes have not in large numbers wandered away from the land of their birth. What the migrants themselves think about it, goes to the very heart of the trouble. Some say that they left the South on account of injustice in the courts, unrest, lack of privileges, denial of the right to vote, bad treatment, oppression, segregation or lynching. Others say that they left to find employment, to secure better wages, better school facilities, and better opportunities to toil upward." Woodson cites *The Crisis*, July 1917, as a source.

41. Regarding the three specific cities, Lawrence might have referred to Scott's study, *Negro Migration During the War*, which had chapters on St. Louis and Chicago; Lawrence himself was from New York.

42. Montaged images of crowds of people moving left, right, back, and toward the front were common in the films of the 1920s; one thinks of Sergei Eisenstein's *Potemkin* (USSR, 1920) and *Strike* (USSR, 1925).

43. Scott, *Negro Migration During the War*, 53, made the point that during the war northern white workers moved to higher-paid jobs in munitions plants, leaving a gap in the ranks of the common laborers.

44. Lawrence recalled in June 1992 that this scene was intended to represent the view from the window.

45. Milton W. Brown, in the essay for the first major retrospective exhibition of Lawrence's work, was the first to point out that these captions must only be thought of as texts "for which the picture is a visual equivalent or symbol, rather than a literal illustration." See Wheat and Brown, *Lawrence*, 11.

46. In the *Migration* series—unlike the *Harriet Tubman* series, where he drew primarily on two written sources—Lawrence drew on many sources for his captions. Du Bois in his various writings for *The Crisis* mentioned aspects of the migration that turn up in Lawrence's imagery.

47. I had the good fortune to look at these panels with Jeffrey Stewart as they hung at The Phillips Collection in June 1992; I am grateful to him for pointing out the billy club.

48. Lawrence, conversation with author, February 27, 1993.

Jacob Lawrence with *Migration* series panel 44, ca. 1941. Lawrence mixed his own colors; he did not use the commercially produced paints shown in this photograph (National Archives, Harmon Foundation Collection).

Precision and Spontaneity:
Jacob Lawrence's Materials and Techniques

ELIZABETH STEELE AND SUSANA M. HALPINE

Jacob Lawrence's economy of line and color are a particularly striking feature of his *Migration* series. He says about his process, "I am not the kind of person to drag a painting out. I work direct."[1] His success in obtaining such charged depictions of the African American migration north derives from his individualistic use of materials and his unique approach to technique, both of which he manipulates to suit the series format. Undertaking a work of art composed of sixty parts forced Lawrence to proceed methodically, yet the images appear spontaneous, full of movement and action.[2] His choice of a fast-drying medium, casein tempera, suits his ability to capture the essence of a moment with limited means. The result is a narrative that is both expressive and forceful.

Lawrence executed the series on standard-size, eighteen-by-twelve-inch hardboard panels that he bought from a local supplier. His choice of support was based on both size and cost.[3] Dimension and shape were also in Lawrence's mind when he envisioned exhibiting the paintings as an entity; alternating horizontal and vertical formats would give the work of art "a certain interest, a certain rhythm."[4] With the help of his wife Gwen, he prepared the smooth side of the panels with a gesso of rabbit-skin glue and whiting.[5] Working on the floor and on a table made of two sawhorses and a board, they brushed three or four coats of the preparation layer across the surface of the panels and then sanded them smooth when dry.[6] Lawrence humorously recalls preparing all the panels at once, despite the large number involved: "You know, when you're young these things go very fast."[7]

The preparation layer has a profound influence on the appearance of the paintings. Viewed under high magnification, a dense matrix of air bubbles is visible in the gesso, causing this layer to be very porous. As paint is

Fig. 1. Photomacrograph of patch of grass (center), middle ground of panel 39. Pinpoint voids in the preparation layer, visible as tiny white dots, give texture to the paint film.

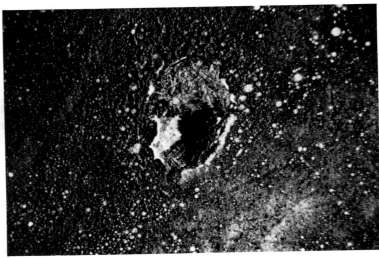

Fig. 2. Photomacrograph of pinhole, upper right corner of panel 51, where preparatory drawing was attached to the prepared surface. Pinpoint voids in the ground layer are also visible as tiny white dots surrounding the pinhole.

brushed across the ground layer, it is drawn into a surface pitted with tiny voids, causing white dots to appear in the paint film; these dots are particularly noticeable in the darker passages (figs. 1, 2). Since gesso grounds are traditionally uniform and smooth in texture, the cause of this extremely porous, pitted surface is of interest. Artists' handbooks warn that air bubbles may develop if the glue solution is too dilute or too concentrated, if it is stirred too vigorously, or if it is prepared in a cold or damp room.[8] One text advises that the gesso should never "stand over hot water a second longer than is absolutely necessary or you will find your gesso full of air bubbles."[9] The air bubbles in Lawrence's panels are probably due to a combination of factors: the need to prepare a large number of panels may have led him to dilute his recipe; the time involved may have meant the gesso sat on a hot burner for a long period; or environmental conditions may have played a part (Gwen Lawrence recalls the West 125th Street studio being without heat).[10] Both the *Frederick Douglass* and the *Harriet Tubman* series of 1938–40, which are painted in the same medium, have gesso grounds that exhibit the same surface characteristics.[11] When asked if he developed the porous ground to create a certain effect such as a fresco-type surface, Lawrence replied that the effect was not intentional. However, pointing to an area in one panel in which the pinpoint white dots were prevalent, he remarked, "if I see something happening which I like, I let it happen. . . . If I got something going like this and I liked it, I let it stay."[12] This improvisational approach to his materials is a key aspect of his process.

Lawrence made preparatory drawings for his compositions (location unknown). Pinholes in all four corners of the panels attest that he affixed the drawings to the panels and then traced onto the gesso (fig. 2).[13] He does not recall the exact method he used to transfer them, but the result is a rather faint underdrawing with the deposit of meager amounts of graphite (fig. 3).[14] Lawrence traced only the larger sections of his drawings, then sometimes added the details freehand with a graphite pencil or often let the development of specifics wait until the painting stage. He explained his rationale: "You can get some nice things going that way . . . you can trace a thing almost exactly as it is and it falls dead. It's flat."[15] His underdrawing was to serve only as a framework for the freedom of his exploration in paint. Lawrence's inventiveness in the absence of a completely

Fig. 3. Close-up infrared photograph of underdrawing for the knot in the sack, panel 39. The evenness and lack of hesitation in the line indicate that it resulted from some type of transfer technique rather than from freehand drawing. Below the knot, faint freehand underdrawing is also present, used to loosely suggest the sack.

worked-up underdrawing is vividly experienced in the woman's garment in panel 53 (fig. 4). Although the general shape of the coat is established, there is no underdrawing for the expressive swirls of the brush that capture the essence of the exotic fur and boa.

Lawrence conceived of the series as a single work of art, not as sixty individual paintings. It was of paramount importance to him that the panels retain a unity, for he feared that if he "executed each panel separately . . . I would maybe feel different from the sixtieth panel than I would from the first."[16] Therefore, he systematically worked on the sixty panels simultaneously. Starting with the darkest color, black, he painted in all the blacks on each panel. He went on to complete the series by moving from the darker values

Fig. 4. Close-up of woman's coat, panel 53. Lawrence painted directly on the panel, with no underdrawing, to arrive at the swirling brush strokes that succinctly capture the essence of the exotic garment.

Lawrence does not use tempera in the traditional technique, modeling shapes by placing individual, small brush strokes side by side in the manner of the fifteenth-century Renaissance artist Carlo Crivelli, whose work he admired.[20] Nor does he create volume by building up thin layers of paint as did his contemporaries Romare Bearden and Ben Shahn, who were also using aqueous media at that time. Instead, he generally paints in one layer, and he achieves a sense of movement and space with his strong sense of line and by varying his brushwork and juxtaposing flat, opaque passages next to more transparent ones or areas in which his brushwork is expressive. This great range is evident in panel 11, where Lawrence varies the textural qualities of his paint to contrast forms and elicit a mood. The woman, child, and table are painted in uniformly applied thick paint with no evident brush strokes. In a single line, Lawrence is able to convey the asymmetrical tilt of the sharply shifted shoulders of the woman as she uses all her weight to cut through the thick slab of fatback. The figures are set off in space by the vibrant brushwork on the green wall behind them. This spontaneous, expressive manipulation of the green paint, which has a life of its own, places the mood of the scene as a serious one. The simplicity and severity of the wood floor is effectively rendered using a dry brush technique, a device Lawrence skillfully employs throughout the series to describe certain textures.

Lawrence's command of aqueous media is clear in his capacity to push the limits of the casein tempera. He describes his own working method as a "mechanical process" in which invention and creativity enter into the development of an image.[21] Reflecting on the second-nature aspect of his technique and his intuitive response to composition, Lawrence rejects the notion of complexity: "You have a feeling for space. You have a feeling for design. I think people do the same things in their homes: If you decorate a room you don't put everything on one side, even if you've never gone to art school: Without even knowing the term design you have a feeling for space, color, texture."[22] Lawrence knows remarkably well how to get the most from a medium that does not accommodate changes and cannot be worked on the surface. In panel 5, he succinctly depicts the headlight of the train as it penetrates the night sky by abruptly changing the tone of the sky from a dark to a light blue. Through his manipulation of the paint he

to the lighter, applying each color to all the panels in succession.[17] His pure colors—ivory black, brown umber, yellow ochre, vermilion, ultramarine, viridian, cadmium orange, and cadmium yellow—are all easily identifiable on sight. Lawrence prepared batches of casein, generally using a single pigment for each color with little mixing to obtain different hues.[18] He sometimes mixed white with blues and greens to obtain different shades of these colors, but these colors are the exceptions and not the rule. Lawrence's systematic approach was again at work in his conscious choice of unmixed colors, which enabled him to make the series a unit by keeping his tones consistent from panel to panel without having to prepare large amounts of paint at a time.[19]

Fig. 5. Close-up of train headlight, panel 5. By varying his brushwork and paint application, Lawrence effectively rendered the appearance of a light piercing the dark sky.

conjures up the misty quality of the light by emphasizing the brush strokes in the conical area lit by the headlight and leaving the surrounding evening opaque and flatly painted (fig. 5). In panel 51, he impulsively achieves a violence in the flames that burst from the windows by using long, single, unbroken brush strokes in black and primary colors. The quick-drying casein tempera obliged Lawrence to get his meaning down quickly in the forceful, individual lines whose bright color sharply contrasts with the gray buildings.

Lawrence was obviously confident of his technique. In his application of paint, spontaneity and chance have equal weight with his systematic working method. The surface textures and shapes are at once intuitive developments and the consequence of working within the limitations of the medium. His paintings reflect a striking absence of changes. He is extraordinarily adept at translating feelings and

portraying moments with economy of means in a fast-drying aqueous medium, manipulating it to fit his precise yet improvisational reaction to color, line, and texture.

NOTES

We would like to thank staff members of the Conservation Department, National Gallery of Art, Washington, D.C., for their kind assistance in writing this essay. In particular, we would like to thank E. René de la Rie, Sarah Fisher, and Catherine Metzger for facilitating the technical examination of the paintings. Finally, we are extremely grateful to Elizabeth Hutton Turner for her steadfast encouragement.

1. Lawrence, interview with authors, Elizabeth Chew, and Shelley Wischhusen-Treece, The Phillips Collection, Washington, D.C., June 4, 1992 (hereafter interview, June 4, 1992).
2. Lawrence, interview with Elizabeth Hutton Turner, Seattle, Washington, October 3, 1992 (hereafter interview, October 3, 1992).
3. Interview, June 4, 1992.
4. Interview, October 3, 1992.
5. Because of the likelihood that a proteinaceous binder was used, medium identification of the preparatory layer using amino acid analysis was undertaken by Susana Halpine, biochemist in the Scientific Research Department at the National Gallery of Art, Washington, D.C. (figs. 6,7). Small samples (2–4 micrograms) were taken by Elizabeth Steele from the edges of the supports for analysis. Amino acid analysis involves first breaking down the proteins in the binders into their constituent amino acids and then matching the amino acid composition with known materials. All samples underwent a water extraction to separate the water-soluble proteins (supernatant) from the water-insoluble proteins and insoluble pigments (precipitate). The extraction is done before the hydrolysis so that the mixtures or adjoining layers of proteinaceous materials can be more clearly characterized. Hydrochloric acid in vapor phase is used to hydrolyze, or break down, the samples. The free amino acids must then be labeled with a specific reagent in order to distinguish them from other organic materials. Therefore, the samples, now containing free amino acids, are derivatized with phenylisothiocyanate (PITC) according to the Picotag protocol developed by the Waters Division, Millipore Corporation. After the phenylthiocarbamyl-amino acids are formed, they are separated and quantitated using high-pressure liquid chromatography (HPLC). The resulting percent composition of the samples is compared with the composition of known materials, such as animal glue, casein, egg yolk, and egg white. Animal glue is characterized by 10% hydroxyproline, 30% glycine, and approximately a 1:8 ratio of serine-to-glycine. The analytical results of the preparation layer were very clear. The amino acid composition of the ground matched that of animal glue, with 10% hydoxyproline and 30% glycine. For further information, refer to the in-house report by Halpine, Scientific Research Department, National Gallery of Art, Washington, D.C., file date August 11, 1992.
6. Interview, June 4, 1992; interview, October 3, 1992. Ellen Harkins Wheat also described Lawrence's preparation of the panels in *Jacob Lawrence, American Painter* (Seattle: University of Washington Press and Seattle Art Museum, 1986), 60–61.
7. Interview, June 4, 1992.
8. Ralph Mayer, *The Artist's Handbook of Materials and Techniques* (New York: Viking Press, 1940), 270. In the June 1992 interview, Lawrence recalled owning both Ralph Mayer's book and Max Doerner's *The Materials of the Artist and Their Use in Painting* (New York: Harcourt, Brace, 1934). However, he believed he got his gesso recipe from another artist rather than from an artist's handbook.
9. Daniel V. Thompson, Jr., *The Practice of Tempera Painting, Materials and Methods* (New Haven: Yale University Press, 1936), 27.

Fig. 6. Chromatograms showing amino acid analysis results of animal glue in gesso ground sample no. 1 from panel 59 (fig. 6a) and rabbit-skin glue reference sample (0.8 micrograms) (fig. 6b).

Fig. 7. Chromatograms showing amino acid analysis results of casein paint in dark brown paint sample no. 2 from panel 39 (fig. 7a) and casein reference sample (2.0 micrograms) (fig. 7b).

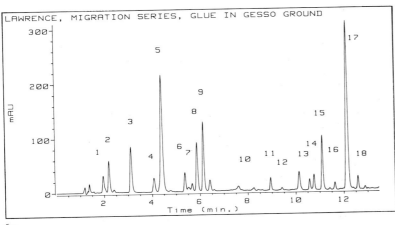

6a

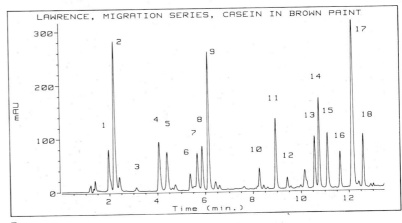

7a

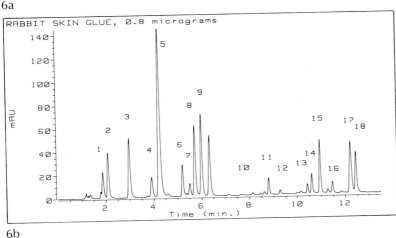

6b

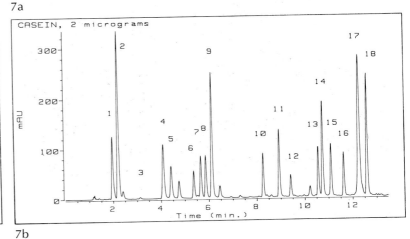

7b

Key

1: aspartate; 2: glutamate; 3: hydroxyproline; 4: serine; 5: glycine; 6: arginine; 7: threonine; 8: alanine; 9: proline; 10: tyrosine; 11: valine; 12: methionine; 13: isoleucine; 14: leucine; 15: norleucine, internal standard; 16: phenylalanine; 17: reagent; 18: lysine.

10. Interview, October 3, 1992.
11. Wheat, *Lawrence*, 46.
12. Interview, June 4, 1992.
13. Interview, June 4, 1992. On each panel there are nearly identical pinholes in approximately the same locations with accompanying loss of ground and paint. Examination under high magnification reveals that the wood fibers in the hardboard are swollen and protrude forward from the surface and that, in numerous instances, paint used on the borders lies deep inside the pinholes. It appears that when the preparatory drawing was removed from the prepared panel, a hole was made in the gesso; however, there initially was no significant loss. When Lawrence painted the border, water went into the pinholes, causing the wood fibers to swell, which in turn caused the gesso to lift and eventually flake from the surface. This occurred early in the history of the panels, since a 1941 installation photograph from the Downtown Gallery exhibition shows the losses. Lawrence said that he felt the pinholes were part of the history of the panels and that the losses should not be restored but left visible. In the same vein, Lawrence did not feel it was necessary to retouch every minor blemish his pictures had suffered over the years. He felt restoration was

advisable only if a damage or scratch had become a source of insecurity or if it broke up his form visually.
14. Although his exact transfer technique is not known, it probably involved rubbing the back of the preparatory sheet with graphite and then pressing the main elements from the front of the drawing onto the gessoed surface. His process resulted in no hesitation or unevenness as there would be in a freehand drawing; rather, the lines are smooth and uniform, with a deliberate feel and little overlapping at intersections.
15. Interview, June 4, 1992; Lawrence, telephone conversation with Elizabeth Steele, November 19, 1992.
16. Interview, October 3, 1992.
17. Interview, June 4, 1992; Wheat, *Lawrence*, 40.
18. Interview, June 4, 1992. Medium identification was carried out on the paint by Susana Halpine using the analytical method described in n. 5. The composition of the paint layer matched that of casein, with 20% glutamate and 14% proline.
19. Ibid.
20. Ibid.
21. Ibid.
22. Ibid.

Chronology
Jacob Lawrence and the *Migration* Series

STEPHEN BENNETT PHILLIPS

1917

September 7: Jacob Lawrence is born in Atlantic City, New Jersey, as thousands of African Americans are migrating from the South to the industrial North. This massive shift is brought about by social and economic factors including the fear of violence, the scourge of the boll weevil, the lack of political power, and segregation and discrimination. The migrants hope for high-paying jobs in such cities as New York, Pittsburgh, Chicago, Indianapolis, and Detroit, where industry is gearing up for war. Most are young, unmarried, and unskilled.

1918

Carter G. Woodson's *A Century of Negro Migration* is published.

1919

Lawrence's family moves to Easton, Pennsylvania; his sister Geraldine is born.

1920

Emmett J. Scott's *Negro Migration During the War* is published; it is probably a source for Lawrence's *Migration* series of 1940–41.

1924

Lawrence's parents are separated. His mother moves with the children to Philadelphia, and a third child, William, is born.

1925

In "Harlem: Mecca of the New Negro," published in *Survey Graphic* (March 1), critic and writer Alain Le Roy Locke identifies a profound new pride, independence, and intolerance of bigotry in African Americans who move north. The same issue points to Harlem as the center of the African American world.

1930

Harlem has the largest concentration of African Americans in the country and is home to 72 percent of African Americans in New York City. According to the 1930 U.S. Census, 87,417 African Americans moved into the community between 1920–30, while 118,792 whites left. When annexed as part of the city in 1873, Harlem was populated by older residents who wanted to escape the noise and new immigrants of lower New York. With the extension of the subway into Harlem in the 1890s, a real estate boom began. But by 1904 the area was overbuilt and overpriced; banks stopped making loans and foreclosed on mortgages. Some landlords started renting to African Americans, who traditionally paid higher prices. Soon Harlem attracted people from established African American sections as well as southerners. Many African American churches moved from Manhattan to Harlem; by becoming the largest African American property owners, the churches helped transform Harlem to an African American neighborhood. By the mid-1920s the headquarters of most New York City African American institutions—fraternal orders, social service agencies, and churches—had moved to Harlem.

1930–31

Lawrence moves to Harlem and lives in the upper 130s and 140s between Lenox and Seventh avenues near Striver's Row. He attends Frederick Douglass Junior High School and the day-care program at Utopia House, where he studies arts and crafts with Charles Alston, who becomes a mentor.

1931

Alain Locke publishes "The American Negro as Artist," in which he states that a unique African American aesthetic sensibility could be translated into art.

1932

Lawrence again studies with Charles Alston, this time at the Harlem Art Workshop at the New York Public Library's 135th Street Branch. He continues there until 1934, when he starts working at Alston's studio, which is home to the WPA Harlem Art Workshop. For a small fee, he is able to remain there until 1940.

1936

Lawrence sees W.E.B. Du Bois's play *Haiti* at the Lafayette Theater. He begins extensive research on the topic at the Schomburg Collection of the 135th Street Branch Library in preparation for his *Toussaint L'Ouverture* series, the first of his many historical narrative series. The series would be completed in 1938 and consists of forty-one paintings depicting the important episodes in Haiti's fight for independence.

The 135th Street Branch—a resource for many of Lawrence's narratives, including the *Migration* series—opened in 1905 to serve a twenty-block area of Harlem. It played an important role in acculturating southern migrants. In 1925 the Division of Negro History, Literature, and Prints was inaugurated, and the next year the New York Public Library, with the help of the Carnegie Foundation, purchased Arthur Schomburg's collection of books, manuscripts, and artwork for the division, making it the world's largest collection of materials relating to African Americans.

Lawrence is awarded a scholarship to the American Artists School, 131 West 14th Street, New York, where he receives his first academic training outside Harlem. He studies there until 1938 under artists such as Harry Gottlieb, Louis Lozowick, and Anton Refregier.

1937

Lawrence's work is exhibited for the first time when six pencil drawings are on view at a Harlem Artists Guild group show at the 135th Street Branch Library in April. Another group exhibition follows at the American Artists School.

1938

At the insistence of Augusta Savage, an African American artist and teacher at the Harlem Art Workshop, Lawrence is hired by the WPA Federal Art Project. He stays for eighteen months, completing an average of two paintings every six weeks. In February, Lawrence has his first one-person exhibition at the Harlem YMCA.

June 10: Arthur A. Schomburg dies. Since 1932 he had presided over his collection at the 135th Street Branch Library. In October 1939 the Division of Negro History, Literature, and Prints is renamed the Schomburg Collection of Negro History and Literature.

1938–39

As part of the Federal Art Project, Lawrence paints the *Frederick Douglass* series, thirty-three narrative panels depicting the life of the Maryland slave turned abolitionist, speaker, and writer.

1939

Lawrence has his first one-person show outside Harlem when the *Toussaint L'Ouverture* series is exhibited at the De Porres Interracial Council headquarters on Vesey Street.

February: "An Exhibition of Contemporary Negro Art" is presented at the Baltimore Museum of Art in cooperation with the Harmon Foundation, an organization supporting the development of African American art. Lawrence's *Toussaint* series has a room of its own.

1939–40

As part of the Federal Art Project, Lawrence paints the *Harriet Tubman* series, thirty-one narrative panels documenting the life of the great conductor on the Underground Railroad.

1940

Alain Locke's *The Negro in Art: A Pictorial Record of the Negro Artist and of the Negro Theme in Art* is published; it includes the work of Jacob Lawrence.

In the spring Lawrence writes Locke asking for a reference in support of his fellowship application to the Julius Rosenwald Fund: "My proposed plan of work is to interpret in a sufficient number of panels (from 40 to 50—18 × 12 [inches]) the great Negro migration north during the World War. I think this will make a colorful and interesting work, as any group migration is in itself."[1]

April 17: Lawrence is awarded a $1,500 fellowship, which allows him to rent his first studio for $8 a month in a loft building occupied by other artists at 33 West 125th Street. From 1940–41 he conducts research in the Schomburg Collection and paints the sixty panels of the *Migration* series. In preparing and gessoing the panels Lawrence enlists the help of Gwendolyn Knight, an artist he met at the Harlem Community Art Center.

1941

Twelve Million Black Voices: A Folk History of the Negro in the United States is published, with text by Richard Wright and photo editing by Edwin Rosskam. It contains nearly 150 photographs from the Farm Security Administration.

June 9: Edith Gregor Halpert, founder of the Downtown Gallery, writes Locke praising his book *The Negro in Art*. She proposes "to introduce Negro art in a large inclusive exhibition . . . following the outline in your book, but limiting it entirely to the work of American Negroes of the Nineteenth and Twentieth century." Locke responds, "Have you seen the work of Jacob Lawrence? I can and will bring along some photographs."[2]

July 24: Lawrence marries Gwendolyn Knight. They travel to New Orleans, their first trip south. While there Lawrence paints the *John Brown* series, twenty-two panels depicting the story of the man whose raid on Harper's Ferry, West Virginia, helped bring about the Civil War. This project is supported by a $1,200 renewal of his Rosenwald Fund fellowship.

August 13: Halpert writes Lawrence in New Orleans to report that *Fortune* magazine is interested in publishing part of the *Migration* series; she expresses interest in having her gallery represent him.

October: Lawrence writes to Halpert: "I have finally decided not to break up the [*Migration*] series. I have reached this conclusion because the complete story was conceived within the sixty paintings; therefore to sell any one painting out of the set would make it an incomplete story. I also know the difficulty of selling the entire set as a whole. I have fixed a price of $2000 for the complete set."[3]

November: *Fortune* publishes a color portfolio of twenty-six panels of the *Migration* series, with text. The Downtown Gallery commemorates the event by exhibiting the series in its main gallery.

December 8: The "American Negro Art" exhibition planned by Halpert and Locke, which includes the *Migration* series, opens at the Downtown Gallery. The gala celebration is overshadowed by the attack on Pearl Harbor the previous day.

Locke writes Lawrence to report that the exhibition "was beautifully set up, and was quite an artistic success. . . . Your work was very much admired; . . . and there are several interested sources for the *Migration* series. With patience I believe they will be sold intact. Mrs. Halpert is conscientious about your interest. She wants you as one of her regular artists, and I strongly advise you to sign. I do not think you will ever regret it. Mr. Barr of The Modern Museum was in three or four times, and liked the whole show, but particularly your work."[4]

1942

January 17: Halpert writes Adele Rosenwald Levy thanking her for serving as a sponsor of "American Negro Art" and proposing that she purchase half the *Migration* series for The Museum of Modern Art. Halpert says that "a good many authorities in the art world consider the series one of the most important contributions to contemporary art. While institutions and artist were eager to buy single panels . . . we all agreed that it would be an unfortunate idea to break up this extraordinary series. We are considering dividing it into two groups of 30 each. Various visitors and members of the Museum of Modern Art agree with me that at least thirty of these panels should be in the collection of The Museum of Modern Art. Mr. Barr has expressed his enthusiasm for these panels and I have reasons to believe that they will be accepted with great appreciation. We feel that the Museum of Modern Art is the logical institution for this collection and that it would benefit not only the Museum and its public, but the artist and his race."[5]

February–May: The Lawrences visit his family in rural Lenexa, Virginia.

February–March: Adele Rosenwald Levy purchases the even-numbered works in the *Migration* series for The Museum of Modern Art, and Duncan Phillips purchases the odd-numbered panels for the Phillips Memorial Gallery. Each pays $1,000.

February 14–March 3: The *Migration* series is exhibited at The Phillips Memorial Gallery, Washington, D.C.

April 18: The Julius Rosenwald Fund renews Lawrence's fellowship again for $1,200 to paint a Harlem series of thirty genre paintings.

June: The Lawrences return to New York City and reside at 72 Hamilton Terrace, Harlem.

1942–44

The Museum of Modern Art organizes a national tour of the *Migration* series, which travels to: Vassar College, Pough-keepsie, New York (October 1–22); Kalamazoo Institute, Kalamazoo, Michigan (November 1–22); Currier Gallery of Art, Manchester, New Hampshire (December 1–22); Addison Gallery of American Art, Andover, Massachusetts (January 1–31, 1943); Wheaton College, Norton, Massachusetts (March 12–April 2); California Palace of the Legion of Honor, San Francisco (April 16–May 7); Portland Art Museum, Portland, Oregon (May 17–June 7); Crocker Art Gallery, Sacramento, California (September 3–24); Mr. William Hill, Los Angeles (December 12–January 1944); The Principia, St. Louis (January 21–February 5); Indiana University, Bloomington (February 14–March 6); West Virginia State College, Institute, West Virginia (March 20–April 10); Lyman Allyn Museum, New London, Connecticut (April 24–May 15); Harvard University, Cambridge, Massachusetts (May 29–June 19); and Museum of Modern Art, New York (October 10–November 5).

1943

The Lawrences leave Harlem for 385 Decatur Street, Brooklyn. Lawrence is drafted into the U.S. Coast Guard as a steward's mate. He continues painting while in the service.

1944

October 10–November 5: The *Migration* series is exhibited at The Museum of Modern Art along with eight new works from the *Coast Guard* series.

1945

February 11–16: The *Migration* series is exhibited at the Brooklyn YWCA in connection with Negro History Week.

December 6: Lawrence is discharged from the Coast Guard.

1946

Summer: Lawrence teaches at Black Mountain College, Asheville, North Carolina.

1946–47

Lawrence uses a 1945 Guggenheim Fellowship to produce the *War* series, fourteen panels based on his war experience.

1947

Fortune commissions Lawrence to paint ten works depicting conditions in the South after World War II and publishes them in the August 1948 issue with text by Walker Evans.

1948

Lawrence receives the Norman Wait Harris Silver Medal and prize for his entry, *Migration*, in the Art Institute of Chicago's Eighth Annual Exhibition of the Society for Contemporary Art. He produces six illustrations on the migration theme for Langston Hughes's book of poetry, *One-Way Ticket*.

1949–50

Lawrence produces the *Hospital* series during his year of psychiatric treatment at Hillside Hospital, Queens, New York.

1951–52

Lawrence produces the *Theater* series, twelve panels inspired by recollections of the Apollo Theater in Harlem.

1953

Lawrence becomes affiliated with the Charles Alan Gallery and is no longer represented by the Downtown Gallery.

1955–56

After conducting research at the Schomburg Collection, Lawrence produces thirty panels of the *Struggle: From the History of the American People* series, which begins in 1775 with Patrick Henry and ends in 1817 with the westward movement. Sixty panels were planned, taking the series through 1908.

1960

The Brooklyn Museum organizes the first major retrospective of Lawrence's work, which travels to sixteen cities.

1962

The Lawrences visit Africa for the first time.

December: Twenty-four panels from the *Migration* series are exhibited at The Phillips Collection, Washington, D.C.

1966

Lawrence is appointed instructor at the New School for Social Research, New York City; he holds this position for three years.

1969

November 14–December 7: The *Migration* series is part of an exhibition on Jacob Lawrence at St. Paul's School, Concord, New Hampshire.

1970

February 14–March 29: The *Migration* series is included in the exhibition "Dimensions of Black" at the La Jolla Museum of Art, La Jolla, California.

Lawrence is appointed visiting artist at the University of Washington, Seattle. In 1971 he is appointed full professor, and the Lawrences move permanently to Seattle.

1971

July 1–September 27: The *Migration* series is included in the exhibition "The Artist as Adversary" at The Museum of Modern Art.

1972

September 10–October 23: The *Migration* series is exhibited at The Phillips Collection.

1973

Lawrence returns to the historical narrative with the *George Washington Bush* series. Commissioned by the state of Washington, the series depicts the journey of a black explorer across the Oregon Trail to the West Coast.

1976

Lawrence uses the migration theme in the serigraph *The Migrants Arrive and Cast Their Ballots*, part of a portfolio of silkscreen prints by twelve artists to celebrate the Bicentennial.

1982

Lawrence paints another historical theme in the *Hiroshima* series of eight works to accompany a special edition of John Hersey's *Hiroshima*.

December 8–January 16, 1983: The *Migration* series is included in an exhibition of Lawrence's works at the Lowe Art Museum, Coral Gables, Florida.

1993

"Jacob Lawrence: The *Migration* Series" is on view at The Phillips Collection, Washington, D.C. (September 23, 1993–January 9, 1994) and begins a two-year tour.

NOTES

This chronology is based on transcripts of interviews with Jacob Lawrence; the essays in this catalogue; Ellen Harkins Wheat, *Jacob Lawrence: American Painter* (Seattle: University of Washington Press and Seattle Art Museum, 1986); Gilbert Osofsky, *Harlem: The Making of a Ghetto* (New York: Harper and Row, 1966); Elinor Des Verney Sinnette, *Arthur A. Schomburg* (Detroit: New York Public Library and Wayne State University Press, 1989); Jeffrey Stewart, *Harlem Renaissance: Art of Black America* (New York: Harry N. Abrams, 1987); and Gary A. Reynolds and Beryl J. Wright, *Against the Odds: African-American Artists and the Harmon Foundation* (Newark, N.J.: Newark Museum, 1989). In addition, this chronology is indebted to the review and contributions of Jeffrey Stewart and Diane Tepfer.

1. Jacob Lawrence to Julius Rosenwald Fund, Rosenwald Fund Collection, Special Collections, Fisk University, Nashville, Tenn.
2. Alain Locke to Edith Halpert, June 16, 1941, Downtown Gallery Papers, Archives of American Art, Smithsonian Institution, Washington, D.C.
3. Lawrence to Halpert, n.d. [October 1941], Downtown Gallery Papers.
4. Locke to Lawrence re success of Downtown Gallery exhibition, ca. December 1941 or early 1942, Alain Locke Papers, Moorland Springarn Research Center, Howard University, Washington, D.C.
5. Halpert to Mrs. Adele M. Levy, January 17, 1942, Downtown Gallery Papers.

Exhibition Checklist

In 1993 Jacob Lawrence revised his 1940–41 narrative for *The Migration of the Negro*. His original text accompanies the color plates of the series (see pp. 54–127), and his revised text is included in this checklist.

Each painting measures 12 in. × 18 in. and is executed in tempera on masonite. The odd-numbered panels are in The Phillips Collection (TPC); the even-numbered panels are in The Museum of Modern Art (MoMA).

1   TPC   During World War I there was a great migration north by southern African Americans.

2   MoMA   The war had caused a labor shortage in northern industry. Citizens of foreign countries were returning to their native lands.

3   TPC   From every southern town migrants left by the hundreds to travel north.

4   MoMA   All other sources of labor having been exhausted, the migrants were the last resource.

5   TPC   Migrants were advanced passage on the railroads, paid for by northern industry. Northern industry was to be repaid by the migrants out of their future wages.

6   MoMA   The trains were crowded with migrants.

7   TPC   The migrant, whose life had been rural and nurtured by the earth, was now moving to urban life dependent on industrial machinery.

8   MoMA   Some left because of promises of work in the North. Others left because their farms had been devastated by floods.

9   TPC   They left because the boll weevil had ravaged the cotton crop.

10   MoMA   They were very poor.

11   TPC   Food had doubled in price because of the war.

12   MoMA   The railroad stations were at times so crowded with people leaving that special guards had to be called to keep order.

13   TPC   The crops were left to dry and rot. There was no one to tend them.

14   MoMA   For African Americans there was no justice in the southern courts.

15   TPC   There were lynchings.

16   MoMA   After a lynching the migration quickened.

17   TPC   Tenant farmers received harsh treatment at the hands of planters.

18   MoMA   The migration gained in momentum.

19   TPC   There had always been discrimination.

20   MoMA   In many of the communities the Black press was read with great interest. It encouraged the movement.

21   TPC   Families arrived at the station very early. They did not wish to miss their trains north.

22   MoMA   Migrants left. They did not feel safe. It was not wise to be found on the streets late at night. They were arrested on the slightest provocation.

23   TPC   The migration spread.

24   MoMA   Their children were forced to work in the fields. They could not go to school.

25   TPC   They left their homes. Soon some communities were left almost empty.

26   MoMA   And people all over the South continued to discuss this great movement.

27   TPC   Many men stayed behind until they could take their families north with them.

28   MoMA   The labor agent sent south by northern industry was a familiar presence in the Black communities.

29   TPC   The labor agent recruited unsuspecting laborers as strike breakers for northern industries.

30   MoMA   In every southern home people met to decide whether or not to go north.

31	TPC	The migrants found improved housing when they arrived north.
32	MoMA	The railroad stations in the South were crowded with northbound travelers.
33	TPC	Letters from relatives in the North told of the better life there.
34	MoMA	The Black press urged the people to leave the South.
35	TPC	They left the South in great numbers. They arrived in the North in great numbers.
36	MoMA	Migrants arrived in Chicago, the gateway to the West.
37	TPC	Many migrants found work in the steel industry.
38	MoMA	They also worked on the railroads.
39	TPC	Railroad platforms were piled high with luggage.
40	MoMA	The migrants arrived in great numbers.
41	TPC	The South was desperate to keep its cheap labor. Northern labor agents were jailed or forced to operate in secrecy.
42	MoMA	To make it difficult for the migrants to leave, they were arrested en masse. They often missed their trains.
43	TPC	In a few sections of the South leaders of both Black and White communities met to discuss ways of making the South a good place to live.
44	MoMA	But living conditions were better in the North.
45	TPC	The migrants arrived in Pittsburgh, one of the great industrial centers of the North.
46	MoMA	Industries boarded their workers in unhealthy quarters. Labor camps were numerous.
47	TPC	As the migrant population grew, good housing became scarce. Workers were forced to live in overcrowded and dilapidated tenement houses.
48	MoMA	Housing was a serious problem.
49	TPC	They found discrimination in the North. It was a different kind.
50	MoMA	Race riots were numerous. White workers were hostile toward the migrants who had been hired to break strikes.
51	TPC	African Americans seeking to find better housing attempted to move into new areas. This resulted in the bombing of their new homes.
52	MoMA	One of the most violent race riots occurred in East St. Louis.
53	TPC	African Americans, long-time residents of northern cities, met the migrants with aloofness and disdain.
54	MoMA	For the migrants, the church was the center of life.
55	TPC	The migrants, having moved suddenly into a crowded and unhealthy environment, soon contracted tuberculosis. The death rate rose.
56	MoMA	The African American professionals were forced to follow their clients in order to make a living.
57	TPC	The female workers were the last to arrive north.
58	MoMA	In the North the African American had more educational opportunities.
59	TPC	In the North they had the freedom to vote.
60	MoMA	And the migrants kept coming.

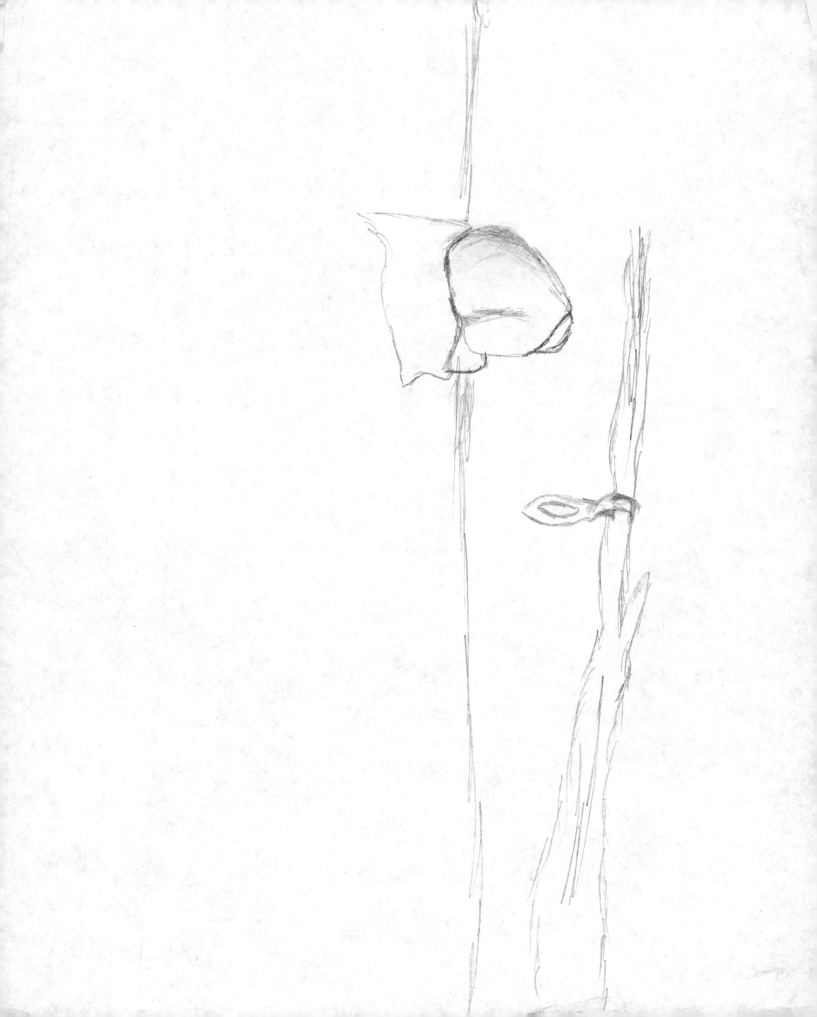

Selected Bibliography

Adero, Malaika. *Up South: Stories, Studies, and Letters of This Century's Black Migration*. New York: New Press, 1993.

Anderson, Jervis. *This Was Harlem: A Cultural Portrait, 1900–1950*. New York: Farrar, Strauss, and Giroux, 1981.

Attaway, William. *Blood on the Forge*. 1941. New York: Doubleday, 1993.

Baltimore Museum of Art. *Contemporary Negro Art*. Baltimore: Baltimore Museum of Art, 1939.

Baraka, Amiri. *Blues People: Negro Music in White America*. Westport, Conn.: Greenwood Press, 1980.

Bearden, Romare, and Harry Henderson. *Six Black Masters of American Art*. Garden City, N.Y.: Zenith Books, 1972.

Bibby, Dierdre. *Augusta Savage and the Art Schools of Harlem*. New York: Schomburg Center for Research in Black Culture, New York Public Library, n.d.

Bontemps, Arna W. *The Harlem Renaissance Remembered: Essays*. New York: Dodd, Mead, 1972.

Brawley, Benjamin. *A Short History of the American Negro*. New York: Macmillan, 1919.

Brown, Jacqueline Rocker. "The Works Progress Administration and the Development of an Afro-American Artist, Jacob Lawrence, Jr." Master's thesis, Howard University, 1974.

Brown, Milton W. *Jacob Lawrence*. New York: Whitney Museum of American Art, 1974.

Brown, Sterling A. *Southern Road*. New York: Harcourt, Brace, 1932.

Bunch, Lonnie. *Black Angelenos: The African American in Los Angeles*. Los Angeles: California Afro-American Museum, 1988.

Burkett, Randall K. *Black Redemption: Churchmen for the Garveyite Movement*. Philadelphia: Temple University Press, 1978.

Crew, Spencer R. *Field to Factory: Afro-American Migration 1915–1940*. Washington, D.C.: National Museum of American History, 1987.

Diner, Hasia. *In the Almost Promised Land: American Jews and Blacks, 1915–1935*. Westport, Conn: Greenwood Press, 1977.

Driskell, David C. *Hidden Heritage: Afro-American Art, 1800–1950*. San Francisco: Art Museum Association of America, 1985.

————. *Two Centuries of Black American Art*. New York: Los Angeles County Museum of Art and Alfred A. Knopf, 1976.

Du Bois, W.E.B. *The Souls of Black Folk*. 1931. New York: Vintage Books, 1990.

Ellison, Ralph. *Invisible Man*. 1952. New York: Vintage Books, 1989.

Embree, Edwin R., and Julia Waxman. *Investment in People: The Story of the Julius Rosenwald Fund*. New York: Harper and Bros., 1949.

Fax, Elton C. *Seventeen Black Artists*. New York: Dodd, Mead and Co., 1971.

Fisher, Rudolph. *The Walls of Jericho*. 1928. New York: Arno Press, 1969.

Franklin, John Hope, and Alfred A. Moss, Jr. *From Slavery to Freedom: A History of Negro Americans*. New York: Alfred A. Knopf, 1988.

Gates, Henry Louis, Jr. *The Signifying Monkey: A Theory of African-American Literary Criticism*. New York: Oxford University Press, 1988.

Goodwin, E. Marvin. *Black Migration in America, 1915–1960*. Lewiston, N.Y.: Edwin Mellen Press, 1990.

Gottlieb, Peter. *Making Their Own Way: Southern Blacks' Migration to Pittsburgh, 1916–30*. Urbana: University of Illinois Press, 1987.

Grossman, James R. *Land of Hope: Chicago, Black Southerners, and the Great Migration*. Chicago: University of Chicago Press, 1989.

Hardy, Charles A., III. "Race and Opportunity: Black Philadelphia During the Era of the Great Migration." Ph.D. diss., Temple University, 1989.

Harlem: Photographs by Aaron Siskind 1932–40. Foreword by Gordon Parks. Introduction by Maricia Battle. Washington, D.C.: National Museum of American Art, 1990.

Heavell, R. H., et al. *Negro Migration in 1916–17*. New York: Negro Universities Press, 1969.

Henri, Florette. *Black Migration: Movement North, 1900–1920*. Garden City, N.Y.: Anchor Press/Doubleday, 1975.

Huggins, Nathan Irvin. *Harlem Renaissance*. New York: Oxford University Press, 1976.

Hughes, Langston. *One-Way Ticket*. Illustrated by Jacob Lawrence. New York: Alfred A. Knopf, 1948.

————. *The Weary Blues*. New York: Alfred A. Knopf, 1926.

————, and John Henrik Clark, eds. *Harlem: A Community in Transition*. New York: Citadel Press, 1964.

Hurston, Zora Neale. *Their Eyes Were Watching God*. 1937. Urbana: University of Illinois Press, 1991.

Igoe, Lynn M., and James Igoe. *250 Years of Afro-American Art.* New York: R. R. Bowker, 1981.

Johnson, Charles S. *The Negro in American Civilization: A Study of Negro Life and Race Relations in the Light of Social Research.* New York: Henry Holt and Co., 1930.

Johnson, James Weldon. *Autobiography of an Ex-Colored Man.* 1927. New York: Penguin Books, 1990.

————. *Black Manhattan.* 1930. New York: Da Capo Press, 1991.

————, ed. *The Book of American Negro Poetry.* 1931. Rev. ed. San Diego: Harcourt Brace Jovanovich, 1983.

Kammen, Michael. *Meadows of Memory: Images of Time and Tradition in American Art and Culture.* Austin: University of Texas Press, 1992.

Larson, Charles, ed. *An Intimation of Things Distant: The Collected Fiction of Nella Larsen.* New York: Doubleday, 1992.

Lawrence, Jacob. Interviews with Elizabeth Hutton Turner. Seattle, Washington, April 13, 1992, and October 3, 1992. Tape transcript, The Phillips Collection, Washington, D.C.

Lemann, Nicholas. *The Promised Land: The Great Black Migration and How It Changed America.* New York: Alfred A. Knopf, 1991.

The Mrs. Adele R. Levy Collection: A Memorial Exhibition. New York: Museum of Modern Art, 1961.

Lewis, David Levering. *When Harlem Was in Vogue.* New York: Alfred A. Knopf, 1981.

Lewis, Samella. *Jacob Lawrence.* Santa Monica, Calif.: Museum of African American Art, 1982.

Locke, Alain Le Roy, ed. "Harlem: Mecca of the New Negro." *Survey Graphic* 51 (March 1, 1925): entire issue.

————. *The Negro in America.* Chicago: American Library Association, 1933.

————. *The Negro in Art: A Pictorial Record of the Negro Artist and of the Negro Theme in Art.* Washington, D.C.: Associates in Negro Folk Education, 1940.

————. *The New Negro: An Interpretation.* New York: A. and C. Boni, 1925.

————. *Up Till Now, The Negro Artist Comes of Age: A National Survey of Contemporary American Artists.* Albany, N.Y.: Albany Institute of History and Art, 1945.

McElroy, Guy C. *Facing History: The Black Image In American Art, 1710–1940.* San Francisco: Bedford Arts Publishers and Corcoran Gallery of Art, 1990.

McKay, Claude. *Home to Harlem.* 1928. Boston: Northeastern University Press, 1987.

McKenzie, Richard D. *The New Deal for Artists.* Princeton: Princeton University Press, 1973.

Marks, Carole. *Farewell—We're Good and Gone: The Great Black Migration.* Bloomington: Indiana University Press, 1989.

Mobley, Marilyn Sanders. *Folk Roots and Mythic Wings in Sarah Orne Jewett and Toni Morrison: The Cultural Function of Narrative.* Baton Rouge: Louisiana State University Press, 1991.

Morrison, Toni. *Song of Solomon.* New York: Alfred A. Knopf, 1977.

Natanson, Nicholas. *The Black Image in the New Deal: The Politics of FSA Photography.* Knoxville: University of Tennessee Press, 1992.

Osofsky, Gilbert. *Harlem: The Making of a Ghetto.* New York: Harper & Row, 1966.

Phillips Memorial Gallery. *Three Negro Artists—Horace Pippin, Jacob Lawrence, Richmond Barth.* Washington, D.C.: Phillips Memorial Gallery, 1947.

Powell, Richard J. *Jacob Lawrence.* New York: Rizzoli, 1992.

Reynolds, Gary A., and Beryl J. Wright. *Against the Odds: African-American Artists and the Harmon Foundation.* Newark, N.J.: Newark Museum, 1989.

Rosskam, Edwin, and Richard Wright. *Twelve Million Black Voices.* New York: Viking Press, 1941.

Saarinen, Aline L. *Jacob Lawrence.* New York: American Federation of Arts, 1960. Reprinted in David Shapiro, ed., *Social Realism as a Weapon.* New York: Frederick Ungar, 1973.

Salzman, Jack, with Adina Back and Gretchen Sullivan Sorin. *Bridges and Boundaries: African Americans and American Jews.* New York: George Braziller and Jewish Museum, 1992.

Scott, Emmett Jay. *Negro Migration During the War.* 1920. New York: Arno Press, 1969.

Sinnette, Elinor Des Verney. *Arthur A. Schomburg: Black Bibliophile and Collector.* Detroit: New York Public Library and Wayne State University Press, 1989.

Stewart, Jeffrey C., ed. *The Critical Temper of Alain Locke: A Selection of His Essays on Art and Culture.* New York: Garland Publishing, 1982.

Stott, William. *Documentary Expression and Thirties America.* New York: Oxford University Press, 1973.

Tepfer, Diane. "Edith Gregor Halpert and the Downtown Gallery Downtown (1926–1940): A Study in American Art Patronage." Ph.D. diss., University of Michigan, 1989.

Toomer, Jean. *Cane.* 1923. New York: W. W. Norton, 1987.

Trotter, J. W., Jr. *Black Milwaukee: The Making of an Industrial Proletariat.* Urbana: University of Illinois Press, 1985.

Wheat, Ellen Harkins. *Jacob Lawrence: American Painter.* Seattle: University of Washington Press and Seattle Art Museum, 1986.

————. *Jacob Lawrence: The Frederick Douglass and Harriet Tubman Series of 1938–40.* Hampton, Va.: Hampton University Museum, 1991.

Williams, George W. *History of the Negro Race in America.* 1883. New York: Arno Press, 1968.

Wintz, Cary. *Black Culture and the Harlem Renaissance.* Houston: Rice University Press, 1988.

Woodson, Carter G. *A Century of Negro Migration*. 1918. New York: AMS Press, 1970.

—————. *The Negro in Our History*. Washington, D.C.: Association for the Study of Negro Life and Culture, 1922.

Wright, Richard. *Black Boy*. 1945. New York: Harper & Row, 1969.

—————. *Native Son*. 1940. New York: Harper & Row, 1969.

Index

Photograph Credits

The text for this book is set in Optima, designed by Hermann Zapf

Composition by The Sarabande Press

Production by Nan Jernigan/The Colman Press

Color separations by Sfera, Milan, Italy

Printing and binding by Sfera/Garzanti, Milan, Italy

Design by Bruce Campbell Design

2   subject   8/00